First World War
and Army of Occupation
War Diary
France, Belgium and Germany

20 DIVISION
Headquarters, Branches and Services
Royal Army Ordnance Corps
Deputy Assistant Director Ordnance Services
22 July 1915 - 31 March 1919

WO95/2104/2

The Naval & Military Press Ltd
www.nmarchive.com
Published in association with The National Archives

Published by

The Naval & Military Press Ltd

Unit 10 Ridgewood Industrial Park,

Uckfield, East Sussex,

TN22 5QE England

Tel: +44 (0) 1825 749494

www.naval-military-press.com

www.nmarchive.com

This diary has been reprinted in facsimile from the original. Any imperfections are inevitably reproduced and the quality may fall short of modern type and cartographic standards.

© Crown Copyright
Images reproduced by permission of The National Archives, London, England, 2015.

Contents

Document type	Place/Title	Date From	Date To
Heading	2104/2 D.A Director Ordnance Service		
Heading	20th Division D.A. Dir. Ordnance Services Jly 1915-Mar 1919		
Heading	70th Division H.Q. 20th Div D.A.D.O.I Vol I Jly to Oct 15		
War Diary	Lumbres	22/07/1915	27/07/1915
War Diary	Lynde	28/07/1915	28/07/1915
War Diary	Merris	29/07/1915	27/08/1915
War Diary	Estaires	28/08/1915	31/10/1915
Heading	H.Q. 20th Div. D.A.D.O.S. Vol 2 Nov. 15		
War Diary	Estaires	01/11/1915	24/11/1915
War Diary	Sailly	25/11/1915	30/11/1915
Heading	D.A.D.S. 20th Div. Vol. 3 Dec 15		
Heading	War Diary of Major Twidale DADOS XXI From Dec 1st 1915 to Dec 31st 1915		
War Diary			
War Diary	Sailly	01/12/1915	16/12/1915
War Diary	Moulle	01/12/1915	15/12/1915
War Diary	Sailly Sur La Lys	17/12/1915	31/12/1915
Heading	D.A.D.S. 20th Div. Vol 4 January 1916		
War Diary	Sailly Sur La Lys	01/01/1916	12/01/1916
War Diary	Steenbecque	13/01/1916	22/01/1916
War Diary	Oxelaere	23/01/1916	31/01/1916
Heading	D.A.D.O.S. 20th Division Vol V		
War Diary	Oxelaere	01/02/1916	03/02/1916
War Diary	Esquelbecque	04/02/1916	12/02/1916
War Diary	Poperinghe	13/02/1916	20/02/1916
War Diary	Eldesdinghe	26/02/1916	29/02/1916
Heading	D A D O S 20 Div Vol 5		
War Diary	Elverdinghe	01/03/1916	17/03/1916
War Diary	Esquebecque	18/04/1916	21/05/1916
War Diary	Poperinghe	22/05/1916	15/07/1916
War Diary	Esquebecque	16/07/1916	20/07/1916
War Diary	Baileul	21/07/1916	24/07/1916
War Diary	Doullens	25/07/1916	29/07/1916
War Diary	Couin	30/07/1916	18/08/1916
War Diary	Beauval	19/08/1916	21/08/1916
War Diary	Treux	22/08/1916	22/08/1916
War Diary	Treux Arbre Fillievres	23/08/1916	31/08/1916
War Diary	Fricourt Distance	01/09/1916	06/09/1916
War Diary	Corbie	07/09/1916	11/09/1916
War Diary	Fricourt Distance	12/09/1916	22/09/1916
War Diary	Treux	23/09/1916	30/09/1916
Heading	D.A.D.O.S. October 1916 Vol 12		
War Diary	Treux	01/10/1916	13/10/1916
War Diary	Corbie	14/10/1916	19/10/1916
War Diary	Vignacourt	20/10/1916	21/10/1916
War Diary	Belloy Sur Somme	22/10/1916	27/10/1916
War Diary	Oissy	08/11/1916	17/11/1916
War Diary	Corbie	18/11/1916	11/12/1916

War Diary	F 11.C. 5.4	12/12/1916	24/12/1916
War Diary	Corbie	26/12/1916	31/12/1916
Heading	War Diary of Capt O R Thana D.A.D.O.S. XX Division From Jany 1st 1917 To Jany 31st 1917		
War Diary	Corbie	01/01/1917	02/01/1917
War Diary	Maricourt	03/01/1917	28/01/1917
War Diary	Heilly	29/01/1917	31/01/1917
Heading	War Diary of D.A.D.O.S. 20th Divn. February. 1917 Vol 16		
War Diary	Maricourt Bois	08/02/1917	28/02/1917
Heading	War Diary of D.A.D.O.S. 20 Division. March 1917 Vol 17		
War Diary	Maricourt Bois	01/03/1917	08/03/1917
War Diary	Maricourt	08/03/1917	13/04/1917
War Diary	Rocquigny	26/03/1917	30/03/1917
Heading	War Diary D.A.D.O.S. May 1917 Vol 19		
War Diary	Rocquigny	01/05/1917	23/05/1917
War Diary	H16. D. 9.5 Near Favreuil	24/05/1917	31/05/1917
Heading	War Diary of D.A.D.O.S. 20th Div June 1917		
Heading	Q20/87/12		
War Diary	Favreuil	01/06/1917	27/06/1917
War Diary	Bernaville	28/06/1917	30/06/1917
Heading	War Diary D A D O S July 1917 Vol 21		
War Diary	Bernaville	01/07/1917	20/07/1917
War Diary	Proven	21/07/1917	31/07/1917
Heading	War Diary D.A.D.O.S. Vol 22		
War Diary	Proven	01/08/1917	05/08/1917
War Diary	A 9.D.3.8 Sheet 28	06/08/1917	19/08/1917
War Diary	Proven	20/08/1917	31/08/1917
Heading	War Diary D A D O S 20th Div Sept 1917 Vol 23		
War Diary	Proven	01/09/1917	10/09/1917
War Diary	A 16 B 3-7 Sheet 28	13/09/1917	28/09/1917
War Diary	Rocquigny	29/09/1917	30/09/1917
War Diary	Fins	15/10/1917	29/10/1917
War Diary	Nurlu	30/10/1917	05/12/1917
War Diary	Hucqueliers	06/12/1917	07/12/1917
War Diary	Blaringhem	08/12/1917	05/01/1918
War Diary	Westoutre	06/01/1918	16/02/1918
War Diary	Blaringhem	17/02/1918	23/02/1918
War Diary	Frevent	24/02/1918	24/02/1918
War Diary	Ercheu	25/02/1918	22/03/1918
War Diary	Beaulieu	23/03/1918	23/03/1918
War Diary	Roye	24/03/1918	25/03/1918
War Diary	Noreuil	26/03/1918	26/03/1918
War Diary	Domart	27/03/1918	27/03/1918
War Diary	St Sauflieu	28/03/1918	28/03/1918
War Diary	Neuville-S-Loeuilly	29/03/1918	29/03/1918
War Diary	St. Sauflier	30/03/1918	31/03/1918
Heading	War Diary of D.A.D.O.S. 20th Div. From 1st. April 1918. to 30th April 1918 Vol 30		
War Diary	Sr Sauflieu	01/04/1918	01/04/1918
War Diary	Briquemesnil	02/04/1918	03/04/1918
War Diary	Liomer	04/04/1918	04/04/1918
War Diary	Lincheux	05/04/1918	09/04/1918
War Diary	Gamaches	10/04/1918	17/04/1918
War Diary	Mingoval	18/04/1918	30/04/1918

War Diary	List of Stores Referred to Under	29/04/1918	29/04/1918
Heading	War Diary of D.A.D.O.S. 20th Division from 1st May 1918 to 31st May 1918 Vol 31		
War Diary			
War Diary	Mingoval	01/05/1918	01/05/1918
War Diary	Villers Au Bois	02/05/1918	05/05/1918
War Diary	Souchez	05/05/1918	31/05/1918
Heading	War Diary of D.A.D.O.S. 20th Division From 1st June 1918 to 30th June 1918 Vol 32		
War Diary			
War Diary	Souchez	01/06/1918	31/08/1918
War Diary	War Diary of D.A.D.O.S. 20th Division From 1st September 1918 To 30th September 1918		
War Diary			
War Diary	Souchez	01/09/1918	05/10/1918
War Diary	Mingoval	06/10/1918	29/10/1918
War Diary	Cambrai	30/10/1918	31/10/1918
Heading	War Diary of D.A.D.O.S. 20th Div. From 1st November 1918 30th November 1918 Vol 37		
War Diary			
War Diary	Cambrai	01/11/1918	03/11/1918
War Diary	Rieux	04/11/1918	04/11/1918
War Diary	Avesnes-Les Aubert	05/11/1918	05/11/1918
War Diary	Vendegies	06/11/1918	06/11/1918
War Diary	Wargnies-Le-Grand	07/11/1918	08/11/1918
War Diary	Bavay	09/11/1918	10/11/1918
War Diary	Feignies	11/11/1918	22/11/1918
War Diary	Cambrai	23/11/1918	28/11/1918
War Diary	Acheux	29/11/1918	30/11/1918
Heading	War Diary of D.A.D.O.S. 20th Division. From 1st December 1918 To 31st December 1918		
War Diary			
War Diary	Acheux	01/12/1918	19/02/1919
War Diary	Amplier	20/02/1919	27/02/1919
War Diary	Doullens	28/02/1919	31/03/1919

2/04/2

D.A Director Aldomana Servo

20TH DIVISION

D.A.DIR.ORDNANCE SERVICES
JLY 1915 - MAR 1919.

20TH DIVISION

20th Hussars

H.Q. 20th Hrs. B.E.F.
Vol I
July to Oct. 15

Confidential

Army Form C. 2118.

WAR DIARY of D.A.D.O.S. 20. Divn. From 21.7.15 to 31.10.15.

INTELLIGENCE SUMMARY

(Erase heading not required.)

Instructions regarding War Diaries and Intelligence Summaries are contained in F. S. Regs., Part II. and the Staff Manual respectively. Title pages will be prepared in manuscript.

Place	Date	Hour	Summary of Events and Information	Remarks and references to Appendices
Lumbres	22.7.15	8. am	Arrived having taken over duties of D.A.D.O.S. 20. Divn on previous day at St. Omer.	Hen K.
"	"	5. pm	A.O.C. personnel (14) arrived. All went into billets.	Hen K
"	23 "	8. am	Smoke Helmets commence arriving. Divn commence to concentrate.	Hen K
"	24 " to 26.7.15	-	" continue " " " " " Divn Continue " " Complete concentration 26.7.15.	
			Went railhead St. Omer each day arranging issue Ordnce Stores. Chief deficiencies in equipment Divn: Infantry 1. Periscopes per unit 2. Sniposcopes " Periscopes " Magazines Enrichmn " Rapid Rect. Sig: " Clinometers Field Various Semi-bren parts.	
"	27.7.15	-	Nothing special to record.	
Lynde	28 "	7. am	Divn moved.	Hen K
Rieurie	29 "	5. am	" - Also went St. Omer to arrange issue of Ordnce Stores.	Hen K
"	30 "	-	" - Shifted railhead to La Gorgue. Also reported personally to D.A.D.O.S. 1st Army Corps.	Hen K
"	31 "	-	Nothing special to record.	Hen K

Date		Time	Entry	Initials
Proceria	1.8.15	—	First big consignment of stores arrived.	HmK
"	2 "	—	Nothing special to record	HmK
"	3 "	11. a.m.	Proceeded to a conference of D.D.O's at 3rd Corps H.Q. Bailleul.	HmK
"	4 "	3. p.m.	D to Hazebrouck afternoon to purchase watering cans. D.A.D.O.S. 1st Army visited my Office.	HmK
			3. Lewis machine Guns redlined to complete 3. Infy; Battns: 15.4 each Supply of Keys having & Lifting Jugs now coming along.	
"	5 "	—	A few spare drums to be also received. Nothing special to record.	HmK
"	6 "	7. a.m. 4.5 p.m	Drove re: filling lines today. Henceforth it will be 5: km daily. Went Pta Gorgue & Hazebrouck re purchase of Lamps, Hand bills & Canvas.	HmK
			5. Lewis m/c; Guns received. 8. Battns now complete. All Lamps Sieges received to complete Infantry.	
"	7 "	—	5. Lewis m/c; Guns received. All 13. Battns now complete. Very large number of Indents dealt with to complete Equipt: today.	HmK
"	8 "	—	Nothing special to record.	HmK
"	9 "	—	D.D.O.S. 1st Army visited my Office.	HmK
"	10 "	2. pm	Do conference of D.D.O's at 3rd Corps. H.Q.	HmK
"	11 "	12. noon	Could not go to Bailhead. Had to proceed Hazebrouck, St. Omer,	HmK
"	12 "	—	Aire & Merville re: purchasing of Boilers to:	HmK
"	13 "	—	Camps. Electric. Signalling now commencing to arrive.	HmK
"	14-15 "	—	Nothing special to record.	HmK
"	17.8.15	—		HmK
"	18.8.15	12. noon	Do conference of D.D.O's at 3rd Corps H.Q.	HmK

Merris	19.8.15	—	To Hazebrouck and Aire on local purchases.	H/nt K
"	20 " and 21.8.15	—	Nothing special to record.	H/nt K
"	22.8.15	—	Long day in office - 15 hours - pulling up back work.	H/nt K
"	23.8.15 to 25.8.15	—	Nothing special to record.	H/nt K
"	26 "	—	Fixed up place h/ Div¹ Arm¹ Shop - Ord¹ Office and Store at Estaires where we move to on 28.8.15.	H/nt K
"	27 "	—	Preparing to move.	H/nt K
Estaires	28 " 8 p.m.	—	Moved to Estaires.	H/nt K
"	29 " to 31.8.15	—	Nothing special to record.	H/nt K
"	1.9.15 to 2.9.15	—	— do. —	H/nt K
"	3.9.15	—	First consignment of Clinometers Field received. Some Spare Arty: Gun Stores + Lewis Mac: Gunstores now arriving.	H/nt K
"	4.9.15 to 5.9.15	—	Nothing special to record.	H/nt K
"	6.9.15	—	Very busy day - but all days are the same. This one especially so. First consignment of 725-0 Blankets arrived, also 745-9 Tube. It melts arrived 8 p.m. and issued next morning.	H/nt K
"	7.9.15	—	Moved into fresh billet nearer my office.	H/nt K
"	8 "	—		H/nt K
"	9.9.15	—	Nothing special to record.	H/nt K

Estaires	10.9.15	—	1. Lewis Mac: Gun received to replace unserviceable.	HWK
"	11 to 14.9.15	—	Nothing special to record.	HWK
"	15 "	—	200. Special Flags, Pink & Green purchased for 3. Infty: Bde:	HWK
"	16 "	—	Nothing special to record.	HWK
"	17 "	—	1. Lewis Machine Gun received to replace "U"	HWK
"	18 "	—	Nothing special to record.	HWK
"	19 "	—	Went to Bethune — Local purchases.	HWK
"	20 to 23.9.15	—	Large consignment of Field Clinometers received. Sufficient to complete Units to half their proportion.	HWK
"	24 "	—	Nothing special to record.	HWK
"	25 "	—	Bag carrying Lewis Machine Gun received for trial and issued to 61. Infty: Bde:	HWK
"	26 "	—	Nothing special to record.	HWK
"	27 "	—	Several urgent demands received from Units for Lewis Mac: Gun parts owing to Gun being in action. Wired board for same and had all outstanding indents for spare parts and components to these guns. First consignment Shade No: 1. Dial Sight rec?	HWK
"	28 "	11. am	18. kr: Gun received to replace 1. U. Took it in lorry to Heavy Mobile Workshop: Merville and handed over to S.O.M. who is issuing a Gun and Carriage to Battery from Reserve held there.	HWK
"	29 "	—	1. Lewis machine Gun received to replace "U"	HWK

Estaires	30.9.15	—	Issue of Smoke Helmets. 2nd pattern. 1st issue to Division of 1. per Officer and man now completed.	HtnK
"	1.10.15	—	Flannellette not obtainable from Base. Old shirting received in lieu and issued. 1. Lewis Mac: Gun received to replace "U" in Lewis Mac: Gun received to replace "U"	HtnK
"	2 "	—	Nothing special to record.	HtnK
"	3.10.15	—	Magazines to Lewis Mac: Guns now commencing to arrive from Base. 20 each received for 10. Battns. Divisional Armourers Shop opened. All outstanding Indicators 3 line now received. 26. issued to 11. different Units. Only previous consignments received were 13 on 7.9.15 and 3 on 16.9.15.	HtnK
"	4. 10. 15 7. 10. 15	—	Nothing special to record.	HtnK
"	8 "	8.a.m.	Proceeded to Boulogne on purchase of Rumbo returning same evening. Further consignment of Magazines to Lewis Mac: Guns received. — 15. each to 10. Battns. Flannellette still unobtainable from Base. Purchased 300 metres of a suitable material locally to issue to troops. (Inty: Battns. and R.E. Field Cos.)	HtnK
"	9 "	—	1. Lewis Mac: Gun received to replace "U". Winter Clothing commenced to arrive. Drawers Woollen, Vests and Bands, Body.	HtnK
"	10 "	—	200 Vermorel Sprayers to 11th Corps. O.D. Vandicourt - Urgent. Nothing special to record.	HtnK
"	11 "	3.p.m.		HtnK
"	12 "	—		HtnK
"	13 "	—	To 3rd Corps. Conference of A.D.O.S.	HtnK
"	14 "	—	Nothing special to record.	HtnK
"	15 "	10.a.m.	To Bethune and Merville on purchase of Hazard Capts. First consignment of Gum Boots arrived. (375)	HtnK

Estaires	16.10.15	10. am	To Hazebrouck on purchase of Hand Carts. 100 Tents C.S. Rec? from Base.	HmK
"	17 "	-	Nothing special to record.	HmK
"	18 "	2. pm	To Hazebrouck + Merville on purchase of Hand Carts.	HmK
"	19 "	-	Arrived at Estaires. Merville as to manufacture of Boot Waistcoats. About 750.	HmK
"	20 " to 24.10.15	-	} Nothing special to record.	HmK
"	25 "	8. am	Proceeded to Bethune and Amiens in connection with purchase of Boot Waistcoats, returning same day.	HmK
"	26 " to 27.10.15	-	} Nothing special to record.	HmK
"	28 "	-	Another consignment of Gum Boots (648) and Winter Clo: received.	HmK
"	29 "	-	Further lot of Gumboots fur (3050) Winter Clo: received, including first	HmK
"	30 "	-	Another consignment of Gum Boots (1186) and Gumboots fur (3000) received. 100 Sets C.S.F: Tent Bottoms rec? from Base.	HmK
"	31 "	-	First consignment of Horse Rugs (1017) arrived.	HmK

Hm Knuttes. Major.
D.A.D.O.S. 20. D.W.

31.10.15.

1794/131

H.Q. 20th Div:
S.A.A.O5
hoi. 2

Nov. 15

4. Sheets.

WAR DIARY of A.D.D.O.S. 20th Divn.
Army Form C. 2118

Sheet 1.   **INTELLIGENCE SUMMARY.** From 1st Nov. 1915.
                                          To 30th " "

Instructions regarding War Diaries and Intelligence Summaries are contained in F.S. Regs., Part II. and the Staff Manual respectively. Title pages will be prepared in manuscript.

(Erase heading not required.)

Confidential

Place	Date	Hour	Summary of Events and Information	Remarks and references to Appendices
Estaires	1.11.15	10. a.m.	Went to Merville: purchase of Bomb Waistcoats. Second consignment of Horse Rugs received. 1 Truck of Ord: Stores for D. in cut off on way up from Havre on 30.10.15. 1 now arrived.	HmK
"	2 "	7 a.m.	Further consignment of Winter Clothing and Horse Rugs arrived railhead — i.e. 2 railway truckloads in addition to one truck of ordinary bulk and detail stores and one truck of vehicles. Bulk consignment of Trenches Jerkins received. 2 Which comprise Water Cart for 11th Durham L.I. and fore part of limbered wagon for Signal Coy. Arranged exchange of 105 Travoys (not reliable to spontaneous combustion, expected to arise shortly) in outbuilding of a house in main street Estaires.	HmK.
"	3 " "	—	Another consignment of Horse Rugs, also 2 nos Machine Gun and mounting for 6th Oxford & Bucks. B.N. to replace one worn out, received. From Lt. R. R.A. Batteries four Range Finders Artillery No.1 received.	HmK.
		3. p.m.	Indents taken of 7th Corps. 20 to be placed as a temporary measure by to D.D. 3rd Corps Troops. Attended conference of D.D.O's of 3 Corps 4th Divn. in	
		12 Noon	next one hour. Went to Merville in afternoon re purchase of Bomb Waistcoats.	HmK.
"	4 " "	4.15 p.m. morning	First consignment of B.6 to T.S received (4o.d). also 600 Copies Map Artois sheet 72. Waiting to claim another 72 Waiting to Carrying formation and 15000 Return Worksheet receiving. Went to Merville and obtained another 3000 Carrying formation.	HmK.

WAR DIARY of D.A.D.O.S. 20th Div:

INTELLIGENCE SUMMARY From 1-11-15. To 30-11-15.

2nd Sheet.

Army Form C. 2118.

Confidential

Place	Date	Hour	Summary of Events and Information	Remarks and references to Appendices
Estaires	5.11.15	7 am	Another consignment of Waistcoats Cardigans received. First issue of 460 Boots to 7.S. 400 pairs made to Infantry from Merville. Also 7000 Waistcoats worsted received. Further consignment of 1000 Boots, gum thigh received by rail. 100 B. gum thigh obtained another 100 Bomb Waistcoats.	HmK
"	6-11	—	Went to Merville & went to Bethune on local purchase of Oil Stores.	HmK
"	7-11	—	Also went to Merville and obtained another 100 Bomb Waistcoats. Another consignment of 5000 Rolls Woollen received for issue to troops. 1000 pairs Boots gum issued to troops in the trenches. Further lot of 333 pairs shoepacks for use of men of R.E. Units in horselines?	HmK
"	8-11	9.30 am	Went Merville; purchase of further Bomb Waistcoats. 333. Shoepacks issued to Infy Bde. 151 Soyer Stoves Read; issue to troops.	HmK
"	"	5 pm	33. Sets of Salvus Breathing Apparatus rec'd. from O.O. 3rd Corps Troops issued to Corps Troops.	HmK
"	9-11	8 am	100 Bomb Waistcoats issued to 61. Infy; Bde; Hd. Qrs. – 30; pairs Boots gum thigh issued to 20. Signal Co. and 10. to A.R.M. for Mil: Police.	HmK
"	10-11	8 am	80 Bomb Waistcoats further rec'd from Merville.	KmK
"	"	11 "	Attended Conference of D.O.D.s at 3rd Corps Hd Qrs.	
"	11-11	8 am	60 Bomb Waistcoats issued to 60. Infy; Bde; 60 to 61st Infy; Bde; 330. Sheepskin Coats rec'd for issue to troops. This completes all due of this Coat. Went Merville for further Bomb Waistcoats.	HmK
"	12-11	—	Large consignment of Horse Shoes received and dealt with. 80. Conferences with final numbers of Periscopes for them received from Base for Infantry Battalions. This completes requirements of the Division.	HmK

WAR DIARY of D.A.D.O.S. 20th Divn.

Army Form C. 2118

From 1-11-15. To 30-11-15.

3rd Sheet.

INTELLIGENCE SUMMARY

(Erase heading not required.)

Instructions regarding War Diaries and Intelligence Summaries are contained in F.S. Regs., Part II. and the Staff Manual respectively. Title pages will be prepared in manuscript.

Place	Date	Hour	Summary of Events and Information	Remarks and references to Appendices
Estaires	13.11.15	-	730 pairs Boots, Gum. Thigh received for issue to men in the trenches.	HMK
"	14."	-	750 Suits Clothing S.D., 650 Puttees, 700 Drawers Woollen and 150 pairs Ankle Boots received from Base for re-clothing 12th K.R.R.C.	HMK
"	15."	-	800 Shirts and 700 pairs Socks issued to 6th K.S.L.I. Large quantities of salvaged Accoutrements, S.A. Ammn, Charges and filled S.A. Cases collected by Salvage Co. being got together for dispatch to Base. First consignment awaits orders to follow.	HMK
"	"	-	4 - 95.M. Mortars received from D.A.D.O.S. 23 Divn. and sent to I.O.M's workshop for conversion to 4"phe: Further consignment of salvaged equipment, S.A. Ammn &c. sent pulkhead for dispatch to the Base. 400 Lantana Tent Folding received from Base for men accommodated in a billets to, where no lighting facilities exist.	HMK
"	16.11.15	-	Went to Merville for further Bomb Waistcoats - also to ascertain go to whereabouts of Nose Bags. Attended 3rd Corps Conference of D.D.O.S.	HMK
"	17."	-	16. Further Gas Strong received. Obtained another 121 Bomb Waistcoats from Merville. 13. Carriage Ambulance, Stretchers arrived from Base for Field Ambulances, but they are emplms as we are complete. Wind Horns as to them dispersed.	HMK
"	18."	-	Obtained a further 110 Pairs of Waistcoats from Merville. This brought to the transaction. Serious shortage of Nose Bags. Very few placed from the Base for weeks past. 2700 due. Wire Dunhill to 3rd Corps for authority to purchase 2000 at 3 Francs 70 cts each.	HMK
"	19."	-		HMK

Confidential

WAR DIARY of D.A.D.O.S. 20th Div:
Army Form C. 2118.

Instructions regarding War Diaries and Intelligence Summaries are contained in F.S. Regs., Part II. and the Staff Manual respectively. Title pages will be prepared in manuscript.

4th Sheet

From 1-11-15
To 30-11-15

Place	Date	Hour	Summary of Events and Information	Remarks and references to Appendices
Estaires	20/11	—	Approval received from 3rd Corps H.Q. to purchase 500 Nose Bags and application gone forward to 1st Army for authority to purchase a further 1500. 500 ordered from R. Remant, Merville. 50. Steel Helmets received from Base. Nothing special to record.	H.K
"	21 "	"		H.K
"	22 "	"	500 Nose Bags L.S. obtained by local purchase at Merville owing to shortage from Base, and another 500 ordered.	H.K / H.K
"	23 "	"	Further 500 Nose Bags purchased at Merville.	H.K
"	24 "	"	Div. HQ. arrived tomorrow to Sailly. D.A.D.O.S. and A.D.O.C. arranged do not move there until tomorrow as A.A.D.O.S. of Div: at present occupying the place does not move until then.	H.K
			First consignment of 2nd Blanket Kurman (1300) received and issued. Divisional Shoemakers also moved to Sailly.	H.K
Sailly	25 "	"	D.A.D.O.S. Offices moved from Estaires to Sailly. Further Blankets arrived.	H.K
"	26 "	"	1165 Boots, Pm, Dub & received from 8th Div: who go into reserve.	H.K
"	27 "	11.a.m	100. Sharping Knives went to Bethune & approved on local purchase. Returned sick. Further 3250 Blankets received.	H.K
"	28 "	"	" 2250 " "	H.K
"	29 "	"	Railhead moved from Lagorgue to Bac St. Maur for 20.Div: also Divis mules received from Base to Bac St. Maur for 20.Div.	H.K
"	30 "	"	150 Steel Trench Helmets received from Base. Also 8. West End Shoemakers from Base. D.O. 20. Corps wrote the record. Nothing special to record.	H.K

H.M.Knobb. Maj.
D.A.D.O.S. 20th Div:
30.11.15.

Astro. de la Stri.
Vol: 3

13/1 1928

Doc 5 Brod

Confidential
War diary
Major Twidale DADOS XX b ⁽ᵂ⁾
from Dec 1st 1915   to Dec 31st 1915

Army Form C. 2118.

WAR DIARY
or
INTELLIGENCE SUMMARY.

(Erase heading not required.)

Instructions regarding War Diaries and Intelligence Summaries are contained in F. S. Regs., Part II. and the Staff Manual respectively. Title pages will be prepared in manuscript.

Place	Date	Hour	Summary of Events and Information	Remarks and references to Appendices

1577 Wt. W10791/1773 500,000 1/15 D. D. & L. A.D.S.S./Forms/C. 2118.

Army Form C. 2118.

WAR DIARY of D.A.D.O.S. 20th Div.

From 1-12-15
To 31 — —

Instructions regarding War Diaries and Intelligence Summaries are contained in F.S. Regs., Part II. and the Staff Manual respectively. Title pages will be prepared in manuscript.

Sheet 1.

INTELLIGENCE SUMMARY

Confidential

(Erase heading not required.)

Place	Date	Hour	Summary of Events and Information	Remarks and references to Appendices
Sailly	1.12.15	12 Noon	Attended 3rd Corps Conference of D.D.O.S.	HrnK
"	"	10 am	4. "West" Bomb Throwing Jacket to 60. Infy. Bde. and 4 to 61. Infy. Bde. yesterday. Went to Estaires on local purchase of stores.	HrnK
"	2.12.15	10.30 am	do.	HrnK
"	3.12.15	10 am	2450 Blankets and 15, Soyers Stoves received from Base. Went Estaires on local purchase of stores.	HrnK
"	4.12.15	11 am	Further consignment of 2900 Blankets received from Base for issue to troops. (2nd Blanket per man). Went to Béthune on local purchase of Electric Light Bulbs for Div. Head.Qrs. Offices. 378. Pairs Gum Boots (Thigh) received over from 8th Div.	HrnK
"	5.12.15	10 am	Went Estaires on local purchase of Stores. Further consignment of 2600 Blankets received from Base, also 250 Steel Trench Helmets received and 800. Nose Rags.	HrnK
"	6.12.15	10.30 am	Went Estaires on local purchase of Rags for carrying in Phono-	HrnK
"	7 "	—	Nothing special to record, receipt 78. Pairs Gum Boots received from 1st Homologation (8. Div) K.Z.	HrnK
"	8 "	12 Noon 2.30 pm	Went to 3rd Corps Conference of D.D.O.S. Went Estaires on local purchase of Laces & Electric Lamps. 22. Pairs Gum Boots received from 1st Home Counties Rd. (8.D. Div)	HrnK
"	9 "	2.15 pm	Went Estaires on local purchase. 12. Pairs Gum Boots received from 8th Div.	HrnK

Army Form C. 2118.

WAR DIARY of D.A.D.D.O.S. 20th Div: from 1.12.15.
INTELLIGENCE SUMMARY. To 31 — 11 —.

Sheet 2.

Confidential

Place	Date	Hour	Summary of Events and Information	Remarks and references to Appendices
Sailly	10.12.15	9.30am 2.pm	Sent Estaires + Merville local purchase of Electric Hand Lamps. 2 DISD Tube pattern Smoke Helmets (2nd Issue Helmet per man) 900. Cap Ko mask stock ands 19. (Handles cooking/4 Lewis machine guns received from Base. 1600 Visits to go thru' which complete the Div: with under teats) and 100. Lanterns, Tent, G.S. fees from Some. Went to Estaires, Merville, Le Thienne, Hazebrouck + St. Omer on local purchase of Gloves, Horns + Gripes.	Appx
— " —	11.12.15	—		Appx

Army Form C. 2118.

WAR DIARY
or
INTELLIGENCE SUMMARY.
(Erase heading not required.)

Instructions regarding War Diaries and Intelligence Summaries are contained in F. S. Regs., Part II. and the Staff Manual respectively. Title pages will be prepared in manuscript.

Place	Date	Hour	Summary of Events and Information	Remarks and references to Appendices
	12.12.15		960 Blankets received from Béne which number completes Division to scale of 2 per man.	
	13.12.15	9.30	Proceeded to Merville to order 100 Kabin bags for experimental purposes. Received 130 pairs short gum boots from S.O. 3rd Corps troops for use in horse lines.	
	14.12.15	10.30	Proceeded to Estaires and Merville to purchase Buck forms, Red Lanterns, - pick up Ration trip. No truck from Béne.	
	15.12.15	9.30	Proceeded to Estaires and Bethune to purchase Electric hand lamps for General Staff. - No truck from Béne.	
	16.12.15		Went to Estaires to purchase Lamps, Oil stove etc - otherwise nothing to record	

Army Form C. 2118.

WAR DIARY
or
INTELLIGENCE SUMMARY.
(Erase heading not required.)

Jo 15 Arj AOAD

Place	Date	Hour	Summary of Events and Information	Remarks and references to Appendices
MOULLE	Dec 1		Jo ARBRICQUES for iron work for OC train. BAILLEUL for lamps. Ordered 250 lamps at HAZEBROUCK.	S'
	2		D.D.O.S. II inspected depot. Death returns received in full 18/600. Jo ERIP Vents ar.d from II Army. Different types hurricane lamps.	S'
	4		Issued Bde HQrs a Imports Zenn[?] lamps.	S'
	5		Jo I Corps workshop for Microclean. Left Kew damaged.	S'
	6		Lt. Sheppard AOD to Bailleul for hurricane lamps [at?] 109. Maj. Larman AOD came from SHQ for instruction in Stores work. Bought 1200 markups from	S'
	9		Jo HQ M.T. Workshops for wagon parts. Jensen for £100.	S' 2AOS I Army 327/1
	10		Working at Capr Macintosh formation of Bde M.S. Corps. This will after 5 BSives only, + Jr Shepd making up. Cap with guns & vehicles.	S'
	11		returned the surplus + guns to Base.	S'
	12		Saw G.O.C. in from.	S'
	13		Prodigious quantity of stores coming up. Searching for apt breech covers. Samples received.	S'

Army Form C. 2118.

WAR DIARY
or
INTELLIGENCE SUMMARY.

D.D.O.
2nd Div.

(Erase heading not required.)

Place	Date	Hour	Summary of Events and Information	Remarks and references to Appendices
MOULLE	Dec. 15		Bought 150 horse rues @ 3.50, & 10000 rifle covers issued. Posted for temporary duty to 20 Div.	8

O'Driscoll Maj. RA.
D.D.O. 2nd Div.

WAR DIARY
INTELLIGENCE SUMMARY.
(Erase heading not required.)

Army Form C. 2118.

D.D.O.
20th Div

Place	Date	Hour	Summary of Events and Information	Remarks and references to Appendices
SAILLY SUR LA LYS	Dec. 17		Joined 20th Div" in relief of Maj Knibbs DSO, on leave orders for the Near East. The Div" seems in good order departmentally. Pde It is in with their Bdes, which visits weekly such requirements the day presents to um. Railhead is at BAC ST MAUR, quite close. Lorries proceed there at 11.30 am daily, unload trucks, return to depot, split up times, load up lorries which form with Supply column, lorries to to regtlemy points & distribute to units. System works well.	
	18		The Armourer shop is in Estaires, & the shoemakers shop is at Sailly. [S] Spare parts for Lewis guns very urgently required. Trench mortar batteries also urgently required. Saw Hand carts for licenced water. & Army Workshops about them. The latter have been instructed to make some.	[S]
	20		Major Knibbs returned 1.0 am & left 8.0 am for Boulogne.	[S]
	26		To DDOS I Army with Capt. Staveley Dale RFA, DAC, to explain about DAC's requirements of harness P&TF's, to complete sets of latter and required in exchange for collar harness, & to replace deficiencies. Arrangement to exchange between 20 + 46" Div.	[S]
	27		To 8th Div to arrange details of move to 2nd area when they move in.	[S]

Army Form C. 2118.

WAR DIARY
or
INTELLIGENCE SUMMARY.

D.O. 20th Div.

(Erase heading not required.)

Instructions regarding War Diaries and Intelligence Summaries are contained in F. S. Regs., Part II. and the Staff Manual respectively. Title pages will be prepared in manuscript.

Place	Date	Hour	Summary of Events and Information	Remarks and references to Appendices
SAILLY SUR LAYS	Dec. 28		Ran to LILLERS to fetch Lt. Evans. AOD.	02
	29		To STEENBECQUE re 8th Div. DOO to make arrangements about them being left behind.	02
	31		To STEENBECQUE. Found a new depot, as the 8th Div. depot is being taken in a Fire Ambulance.	02
			Except from the 27-30 inclusive when it did not rain, the month has been very wet. The Lys is in flood, & most of the country in this neighbourhood under water.	
			An A.D.O.S. 3rd Corps, Major Lannam has been appointed & is at present at Corps HQ.	

O Dugdale Maj. RA
DOO 20 Div

Bishop 23 E Str.
Fol: 4
7th January 1906

Army Form C. 2118.

WAR DIARY
or
INTELLIGENCE SUMMARY.
(Erase heading not required.)

DDS. 20th Divn.

Place	Date	Hour	Summary of Events and Information	Remarks and references to Appendices
SAILLY SUR LA LYS	Jan 1		To HINGES with gas cylinders for refilling. Got at night.	02 S1
	2		To A.D.O.S. 3rd Corps.	S1
	3		Buying belts for warning against gas attack. 1 cross cut saws for wood cutting part	S1
	4		Saw D.D.O.S. I Army & ADOS 3rd Corps.	S1
	5		With Lt Evans to the new area of not. Inspected new depot at STEENBECQUE.	S1
	6		To Divl Baths. Also saw Armourers at 3rd Corps workshops individuals in care of Yeomanic Sprayers.	S1
	7		Lt. Evans telds Pearman to Steenbecque.	S1
	8		ADOS 3rd Corps has a full day with Lt Evans in office. I think he is too quickly starting new ideas – which increases our paper with no material result.	S1
	9		Lt Evans to Steenbecque. closing up at the my doings, as am to arrive as DADOS II Army. Jan 16th	S1

O'Neale Maj RA
DDO 20th Divn

WAR DIARY
or
INTELLIGENCE SUMMARY.
(Erase heading not required.)

Army Form C. 2118.

J. DAWOT
XI Division
January 1916

Place	Date	Hour	Summary of Events and Information	Remarks and references to Appendices
Little camp Jan				
nr top	10	—	Took over duties from Major S. Tisdale on 6 + 9 II Army	
"	11th	—	Went to see H. of Spec. Blanghem in Lille + states received instructions	
"	12th	—	Moved ADMS Office + Hors. to Steenbecque with four lorries	
STEENBECQUE	13th	—	To Bethune to purchase pitch, candles + stones for E. Spec.	
"	14th	—	To Langhemark, local purchase of stores replenishing panniers to ensure	
"	15th	—	Ambulances Divisional Hos. to one at Hondeghem, being Io	
"			To ADOS 3rd Corps + Engelbroucq, and most stores + stores in use and	
"	16th	—	To Conference at 3rd Orders of Quartier	
"	17th	—	To Aire local purchases, large consignment of Whitehead received from	
"			Base. New ordering which secured for Medium this Division	
"	18th	—	To Lillers + Bethune to purchase large consignments also	
"	19th	—	To Langhemarq, local purchase also Hondeghem to find purveyor	
"			outside for new workshop, also Amuntrics & Rlles	
"	20th	—	To Bailleul to purchase 536 Wine colour	
"	21st	—	To Langhemarq to find New Stores etc for a few days as Division on the move	

WAR DIARY
or
INTELLIGENCE SUMMARY.
(Erase heading not required.)

Army Form C. 2118.

DADMS
XI Division

Place	Date	Hour	Summary of Events and Information	Remarks and references to Appendices
STEENBECQUE	22		To Ordnance to arrange Offices & billets for Ordnance staff, also to Hazebrouck re storage of amalgamated units & state of the place	(1)
October	23rd		Headquarters II Army & Army Mobile Workshops	(2)
"	24		11-15.60 H.Q re Travelling Kitchens taken over on march, also to II Army Heavy Mobile Workshops	(3)
"	25		Hazebrouck re handing over surplus stores to DADOS 34th Division	(4)
"	26		To G. II Army & ADOS III Corps re Corps Allotments	(5)
"	27		Hazebrouck re Travellers & Armourers Shops, stores of bicycles, tools etc.	(6)
"	28		DADOS 49th Division in rear area	(7)
"	29		H.Q II Army re the arrangement of supplements regarding bulk issue of cigarettes	(8)
"	30		People to help us reg. 236th Inf. Regt. B.E. Arras. Germans shelling the Place Hôtel de Ville accurately & having regimental office near the Église	(9)
"	31		Petersinghe to arrange Porking car near the suffix of ADOS 14th Division also to H.Q 14th Division near Lynde (?). This Division has been practically more since formed & gunners it.	(10)

R M Thomas. Lt.Col.
DDO XI Division

S. A. S. Q. F.
20d. Division
Vol. V

Army Form C. 2118.

WAR DIARY
or
INTELLIGENCE SUMMARY.
(Erase heading not required.)

DDD
XI Division

Instructions regarding War Diaries and Intelligence Summaries are contained in F. S. Regs., Part II. and the Staff Manual respectively. Title pages will be prepared in manuscript.

Place	Date	Hour	Summary of Events and Information	Remarks and references to Appendices
Oulchie	Sept 1st		To I Army HQ re plans for Embarkation stores	(A)
"	2nd		To Esquerdogne to arrange with DADOS to take over his office + staff	(B)
"	3rd		To new area (Esquerdogne) with Staff office etc. H.Q moved same day	(B)
Esquerdogne	4th		To I Army HQ Workshops. Agreement with plans for Embarkment. Workshops which they are making for the Division. 50 Personal Grease Covers from Boesar for the Division.	
"	5th		To Div I.Q. re course of erection near Ypres to meet AA & QMG	(C)
			re purchasing titles etc for officer.	(C)
"	6th		To field cashier Bailleul — DADOS 34th Division re handing over.	(C)
			Saw sets of entrenching utensils.	
"	7th		To Bailleul Estaires re local purchase. Huge amount of light received from base including first consignment of new Pit Smoke Helmets.	(D)
"	8th		To Boyenghe + 14th Division HQ to arrange with DADOS	(D)
			to take over Stores + Ambulances Cows.	
"	9th		To Hazebrouck. local purchase. First supply of PH Helmets (1400 officers + 1 hr men, issued to the Army, today, complete	(D)

WAR DIARY
or
INTELLIGENCE SUMMARY

Army Form C. 2118.

WOO
20th Division

Place	Date	Hour	Summary of Events and Information	Remarks and references to Appendices
Eysnekhoeye	Sept 10		To Ypres wagon with DADOS of 14th Division to see over his ammunition store & Dept. Saw rest of Station. Two huts being shelled by large range artillery. One shell narrowly missed us.	
— " —	11th		To Pop. Arrived at 8 on the way to Elverdinghe to see Journey of Ammn Station for Offrs in huts also in tents etc.	
— " —	12th		To Elverdinghe to find billets in another. Offrs are to Engineers Coast purchase	
Elverdinghe	13th		Got new stores from DADOS 14th Division. Aeroplane over but no firing at. Elverdinghe all horses bad ups.	
— " —	14th		Another taken ammunition of OC Smoke Helmets in Ypres shelled in the return.	
— " —	15th		To Dunkerque heavy purchase. Aeroplane raid 3 times in the night.	
— " —	16th		Secured mutton also a little fruit but not very much in this shopping in fees adjoining town	
— " —	17th		To Brileul re food purchase. Started on 11500 OA Smoke Helmets. Ypres again shelled.	

Army Form C. 2118.

WAR DIARY
or
INTELLIGENCE SUMMARY
(Erase heading not required.)

O.A.D.D.S.
20th Divisionair

Place	Date	Hour	Summary of Events and Information	Remarks and references to Appendices
Poperinghe	19th		To Dunkerque to purchase large number of primus stoves, none etc. for new Divisional boundary.	(P)
"	20th		Moved HQrs near new site. To Lt G.G. Bear & to Fort 12 No 6. Brigades. Crinsch kind of shells again	or
"	21st		To Longuenesse to meet purchases, have arrangement for fresh of things never kept to received.	
"	22nd		To 14 H Corps Workshops visits Baupre offer.	or
"	23rd		H.Q. to 14 Corps & Bardent to at purchase. German trenches yes.	or
"	24th		To Longuenesse to extranual stores at I Army R G shop.	or
"	25th		Moved Offices to H.Q. on the move to Clevringhe.	(P)
Clevringhe	26th		at I Army Workshops to lift to Black battery also to Outhaut to Torren Rechercher from Chermont attempt.	or
"	27th		to Lt G.O.C. I Army re German orders ore cartridges, also to Supply column re ammu for lorry 18 to 20 th Dunkerque to take Major G3 Divisional Command	

Army Form C. 2118.

WAR DIARY
or
INTELLIGENCE SUMMARY

(Erase heading not required.)

Instructions regarding War Diaries and Intelligence Summaries are contained in F. S. Regs., Part II. and the Staff Manual respectively. Title pages will be prepared in manuscript.

Place	Date	Hour	Summary of Events and Information	Remarks and references to Appendices
Edinburgh	Feb 28th	—	To Dunkirque to purchase materiel for Divisional Ammunity	(1)
—	" 29th	—	To A.D.O.S. 19th Corps, Conference, & time of undertaking recourse from Base for new Divisional Batteries Ret.	(2)

O.K. Brown
O. & D.O.S.
20th Division
29/2/16

DADOS.
20 DW
vol 5
6

Army Form C. 2118.

D.A.D.O.S.
20th Division.

WAR DIARY
or
INTELLIGENCE SUMMARY.
(Erase heading not required.)

Instructions regarding War Diaries and Intelligence Summaries are contained in F. S. Regs., Part II. and the Staff Manual respectively. Title pages will be prepared in manuscript.

Place	Date	Hour	Summary of Events and Information	Remarks and references to Appendices
Eberdinghe	1st		To Wormhoudt re purchasing small stores & boilers &c. Meeting over it in Schocks also morning office in Eberdinghe large amount of equipment received from base for unit Divisional units	(B)
	2nd		To Eberdinghe re purchasing 100 large mattress covers bags for carrying returns to Cassels.	(C)
	3rd		To H. Corps S. D. C. conference with A.D.O.S. Ouwacinghe, obtain details number of returns wanted. Returns commenced.	(C)
	4th		To Eberdinghe re purchasing, visited for G Court into use and furniture up a statement. Court at Infurniere to interview its officers to bring it at & Pl. 3 miles away.	(C)
	5th		To S. of C. 2nd Army travel by car D.D.O.S. re purchase of Iron standards head covers	(C)
	6th		To A.D.O.S. 4th Corps S.D.C. & Ouwacinghe.	(B)
	7th		To Ouwacinghe & Cassels re Relieving certificates for 30 men Pres & Divisional Units.	(B)
	8th		To 2nd Army H.Q. & Hazebrouck re purchasing Foot covers	(B)

1577 Wt. W10791/1773 500,000 1/15 D. D. & L. A.D.S.S./Forms/C. 2118.

Army Form C. 2118.

WAR DIARY
or
INTELLIGENCE SUMMARY.
(Erase heading not required.)

Instructions regarding War Diaries and Intelligence Summaries are contained in F. S. Regs., Part II. and the Staff Manual respectively. Title pages will be prepared in manuscript.

Place	Date	Hour	Summary of Events and Information	Remarks and references to Appendices
Boulogne	9. 9.		Boulogne re purchasing Expedition Absorbent cotton & rifles for trench	(1)
"	10th		To I Army Workshops Wimereux re return for Intrenchments	(2)
"	11th		Cooking Range, Morse Code & new rifles with telescope sights	(3)
"	12th		To I Army & G Cassel & OM Ammunition Amiens for account	(4)
"			Sent ammunition for 1600 Rifles.	(5)
"	13th		B.B. Cast, steele or others, with cutting also A.D.O.S 1st Corps	(6)
"	14		Boulogne re purchasing small trailer returns for trenches	(7)
"	15		To I Army Trench Mortar School, Berthen to show new sights	(8)
"	16		A.D.O.S 1st Corps & Ordnance Workshops	(9)
"	17		Etaplens re local purchase	(10)
"	18		Boulogne re purchasing 400 Ammo collars	(11)
"	19		To G. I Army.	(12)

Army Form C. 2118.

WAR DIARY
or
INTELLIGENCE SUMMARY.
(Erase heading not required.)

DADOS
23rd Division

Place	Date	Hour	Summary of Events and Information	Remarks and references to Appendices
	March			
Chartreuse	20th		Conference with A.D.O.S. 14th Corps re establishment of Mule Clothing	(1)
"	21st		Endeavour to purchase material for Barrack laundry	(2)
"	22nd		Visit to A. Supt. Corpse Hoane. O.C. Salvage by usual Refreshment also Ammunition store. Saw that what is on the trucks from B. Brad in the stocking over new trucks pro- tem status (am empty)	(3)
"	23rd		Huge traffic returning. Extreme Pressure the crews of 11 O.B preceded Extreme retirement order clothing forwarded	(4)
"	24th		Proceeded to England. also Cambridge base, Boulogne over nights to Caire to Caen	(5)

O.K. Sacour
D.A.D.O.S.
23rd Division

Army Form C. 2118.

VOL B

DADVS
20th Division

WAR DIARY
INTELLIGENCE SUMMARY.
(Erase heading not required.)

Instructions regarding War Diaries and Intelligence Summaries are contained in F. S. Regs., Part II. and the Staff Manual respectively. Title pages will be prepared in manuscript.

Place	Date	Hour	Summary of Events and Information	Remarks and references to Appendices
Etaples	8		Reference from England on Cape & Foot over Arthur from Cape Home	
"	9		Visits fitting progress at D.O. Camp, N.S. Mns Horse and yesterday	
"	10		To ADVS 14th Corps & DADVS 6th Division, Boulogne	(1)
"	11		" " " D.I. Army, Cassel	(2)
"	12		" Longuenesse Remount	(3)
"	13		" DADVS 6th & 2nd Division, Boulogne re Estray Mag ride new store	(4)
"	14		" 14th Corps Mobile Vety & GS Workshops, II Army re Louisiana	(5)
"	14		for Remits Front	
"	15		To Boulogne re finding billets, etc for Armour Remounts	(6)
"	16		" ADVS 14th Corps & Longuenesse, Front Purchase	(7)
"	17		" DVS II Army	(8)
"			Moved store of Office to New area at Boulogne	(9)
Boulogne	18		Store up. New store for return of Winter Clothing & Armour Slip	(10)
"	19		To H.Q. II Army re obtaining of new Divices Bestoxmelt rifles	(11)

WAR DIARY
or
INTELLIGENCE SUMMARY.

Army Form C. 2118.

DADOS 20th Division.

Place	Date	Hour	Summary of Events and Information	Remarks and references to Appendices
Boyenberghen	April 20th		Return of OO's over OR Lebruits received from Base	(R)
"	21st		To Stagehouse re local purchase	(R)
"	22nd		To 60th Brigade HQ at Watten	(R)
"	23rd		To Conference at 14th Corps Queen	(R)
"	24th		To 14th Corps Ordnance Workshops	(R)
"	25th		re Obtaining re purchase of 2000 trench rifle covers	(R)
"	25th		To Stagehouse re local purchase	(R)
"	26th		To OBC for civic ferring kits for tertiary explosive at Ordnance Workshops	(R)
"	27th		DADOS II Army	(R)
"	28th		To II Army R.E. Workshops	(R)
"	29th		To Ostend re local purchase	(R)
"	30th		To ADOS re return of all Winter Clothing and further reserve blankets	(R)

O.K. Browne
DADOS
20th Division

30/4/16

Army Form C. 2118.

DA DDS
20th Division

Vol 7

WAR DIARY
or
INTELLIGENCE SUMMARY.
(Erase heading not required.)

Place	Date	Hour	Summary of Events and Information	Remarks and references to Appendices
Boulogne	1st Army		To Controller Food Purchase. Workshop hill.	(?)
"	2nd		To DDOS II Army re contract for furnishing Ordnance Rest Station	(?)
"	3rd		To Department re local purchases	(?)
"	4th		To Base Cashier. 14th Corps re Imprest Account	(?)
"	5th		To DADOS Guards Division re Tents	(?)
"	6th		To Workshops (DAC) + Engineers re boot machine	(?)
"	7th		To Workers to see M.T. of 61st Brigade. Car broke down	(?)
"	8th		Wrote re suitable Enclosure + how to fold long & short arms in	(?)
"	9th		To 59th Brigade HQrs.	
"	10th		To 14th Corps Ordnance Workshops & to see Captain Long supply Officer DADOS of Guards Division	(?)
"	11th		Going to take over from DADOS II Army.	(?)
"	12th		DDOS II Army.	
"			DM Troops at Abbeville & to see Ordnance Reports	(?)

Army Form C. 2118.

WAR DIARY
or
INTELLIGENCE SUMMARY.
(Erase heading not required.)

Instructions regarding War Diaries and Intelligence Summaries are contained in F. S. Regs., Part II. and the Staff Manual respectively. Title pages will be prepared in manuscript.

D.A.D.O.S.
20 Division

Place	Date	Hour	Summary of Events and Information	Remarks and references to Appendices
Reninghelst	13		To II Army H.Q. re Stores for Divisional Workshops	(2)
"	14		" A.D.O.S. II Corps re Stores	(1)
"	15		Ordnance Workshops. II Corps re Ammunition	(2)
"	16		Ripinghe re taking over from French D.A.D.O.S.	(3)
"	17		Equipment for Forest Ordnance	(4)
"	18		D.A.D.C. Remounts re change of Remounts	(5)
"	19		D.D.O.S. II Army H.Q. Cassel	(6)
"	20		Camps K L & M Reserve	(7)
"	21		Copinghe to take over from French Division	(8)
"	22		Ordnance Workshops 14 Corps re Spare Ammunition	(9)
Copinghe	23		To Cassel D.D.O.S. II Army	(10)

Army Form C. 2118.

WAR DIARY
or
INTELLIGENCE SUMMARY.

(Erase heading not required.)

DADOS
20th Division

Place	Date	Hour	Summary of Events and Information	Remarks and references to Appendices
Proven	May 25		Dunkerque re local purchase of oats for Army H.Q. Camp	(A)
— " —	26		ADOS 14th Corps	(B)
— " —	27		Lieutenant O.H. Orm re local purchase of 2500 breast side covers @ 80 centimes each	(C)
— " —	28		Ordnance Workshops re conversion. Covering re Armoury. Called all day too	(D)
— " —	29		Lieutenant re local purchase of Tubs for Laundry	(E)
— " —	30		Conference with 14th Corps Ord	(F)
— " —	31		Dunkerque re local purchase	(G)

O.K. Evans Capt
DADOS
20th Division

WAR DIARY
or
INTELLIGENCE SUMMARY

Army Form C. 2118.

D + D O S
20th Division
Vol 8

Place	Date	Hour	Summary of Events and Information	Remarks and references to Appendices
Cerisy	June 1st		To Ordnance Workshops 16th Corps re Binoculars	
"	2nd		6 З.А. Batteries with A.O.D. re bore gauges	
"	3rd		Overhaul re issue & purchase of Barrel stars	
"	4th		Devis of Bores for 63 18/prs Hotchkiss Bowdens re Cordtend by Enginees	
			Ordered fire when Commenteys on attacks	
"	5th		To D.D.O.S. II Army H.Q. to felet new closed quarters for dept	
"	6th		To this Division. Saw 18 horses issued up from Base	
"	7th		To A.D.O.D. 14th Corps & 5 Field Batteries	
"	8th		Engagement to fetch 1000 wheel rifle covers	
"	9th			
"	10th		To Engineers re 10 days leave	
"	11th		To A.D.O.S. 14th Corps. Eng attach & Germans answerk'se	
"	17th		To A.D.O.S. 14th Corps. Artillery duel.	

WAR DIARY

INTELLIGENCE SUMMARY

Army Form C. 2118.

DADOS
20th Division

(Erase heading not required.)

Place	Date	Hour	Summary of Events and Information	Remarks and references to Appendices
Peronne	Sept 18		Despatched to Est. 1000 head rifle covers.	(1)
"	19		Field Cashiers & Ordnance Workshops	(2)
"	20		Divergence re Boot Purchase & making up enough Bootlegs	(3)
"	21		Despatched 50 Boot Purchase	(4)
"	22		VDOS I being with new ASC Food Container	(5)
"	23		ODOS 14th Corps	
"	24		Divergence re Local Purchase of cordless bandage & small	(6)
"	25		Hearts given by me in return for mines [illegible]	
"	26		Returns re Workshops & Salvage Coys	(7)
"	27		Purchase Tin Boxes & similar [illegible] Workshops	(8)
"	28		Stables in use	(9)
"	29		14th Corps Coy	(10)
"	30		[illegible]	

July

Vol 9

WAR DIARY
INTELLIGENCE SUMMARY
(Erase heading not required.)

Army Form C. 2118.

DADS
20th Division

Place	Date	Hour	Summary of Events and Information	Remarks and references to Appendices
Etaples	July 1st	—	To Hazebrouck re local purchase	
— " —	2nd	—	To DADS I Army Cassel, to Mr Indoous Chronicles re	
— " —	3rd	—	To ADOS 14th Corps re new Serjeant Clerk to replace Sgt	
— " —	4th	—	To Somerville proceeding to England to take up a commission. Seventy-two hours leave Leave arriving from Base. 12 for use at Matron hanging ropes for use. Butts up to 8.	
— " —	5th	—	To Ordnance Bolobos	
— " —	6th	—	To Builders re local purchase	
— " —	7th	—	To ADOS 14th Corps	
— " —	8th	—	DADOS Seventh Division also Field packers	
— " —	9th	—	To Dunkerque re local purchase	
— " —	10th	—	To IOM Ordnance Workshops & DADOS Z.	

Army Form C. 2118.

WAR DIARY
or
INTELLIGENCE SUMMARY.

(Erase heading not required.)

A.D.V.S.
20th Division

Place	Date	Hour	Summary of Events and Information	Remarks and references to Appendices
Epéhy	11		Inspected to local purchase. Epéhy Honeychelles	(R)
—	12		A.D.O.S. 14th Corps. Epéhy upon orders of May	(R)
—	13		Inspected B.E.L. Army Workshops. Epéhy stables	(R)
—	14		Ordnance Workshops. About 300 shells found in German Ammo Dump. Numbers tags/marks etc.	(R)
—			Interest Demand to D.O. evacuated some still interest	(R)
—	15		Horse Ammo Dump Stores + Offices at Equancourt 60T Brigade attached to 2 ANZAC Corps. On arrival	(R)
Equillecourt 16			regrouping in the brea.	
—	17		D.D.V.S. I Army	(R)
—			Arrived re local purchase	(R)
—	18		158 R.A.M. by Order of A.G.M. G. 29 4th Division Backed Warmmes Workshops + D.D.V.S. 14 Corps (ammo)	(R)
—	19			
—	20			
Bertincourt			Offered Stores, Offices + Warmmes shops to Bertcoat (14 + Army)	
—			Le Oethuenberto de Rawlinge, via Lettres now sent to the Army	
—			offered 5 DD limbers through Benn to forward to issue, no evacuates	
—			forage 60 Brigade not ADOS 6th Corps.	

WAR DIARY
or
INTELLIGENCE SUMMARY
(Erase heading not required.)

Army Form C. 2118.

DADOS
28th Division

Place	Date	Hour	Summary of Events and Information	Remarks and references to Appendices
Boulogne	July 22nd		L.A.D.O.S. I Corps to handover to 28th Division	(1)
"	23rd		G.R.O. Corps re advance of Divisional Ammunition Columns to [illegible]	(2)
Boulogne	24th		Started our Office Note to 28th Division re supply of MT & LT lorries & artillery	(2)
Vieille [?]	25th		Sirical Ordnance Store Army for number of attachments to replace unserviceable & for troops	(3)
"	26th		To DADOS 12th Division re handing over his state of harness	(4)
"	27th		To DADOS 38th Division re taking over his state of harness	(4)
"	28th		on the 29th inst. Reannexures at [illegible] re relieving 38th Division	(5)
"	29th		Took over office & state from 38th Division	(7)
Hamme [?]	30th		29th & 38th Division Artillery transferred to me for ordnance	(8)
"	31st		stores. Our Artillery transferred to 29th Division for ordnance	(9)

O.R. [signature] Capt
DADOS 28th Division
31/7/16

Army Form C. 2118.

WAR DIARY
or
INTELLIGENCE SUMMARY
(Erase heading not required.)

DADVS
20th Division Vol 16

Place	Date	Hour	Summary of Events and Information	Remarks and references to Appendices
Corbie	1st		To new Quarters Belle Eglise	(1)
"	2nd		To DADVS Reserve Army Hanchard re Artillery units attached to Corps	(2)
"	3rd		To ADVS 14th Corps Mericourt	
"	4th		To DADVS 20th Division Detachment re 29th Division Artillery	(3)
"	5th		To Amiens re Ambulance transport for traffic control	
"	6th		To CO Corps Troops Mericourt re Carts	(4)
"	7th		To field Cashier Corbie & ADVS Mericourt	(5)
"	8th		To DOM re removal re Blanche cognac	(6)
"	9th		To Amiens re purchase of stores for turning details & workshops	
"	10th		To DADVS Hanchard & Army HQ Contramaisnil	(7)
"	11th		To DDVS Fredhillers re changing horses	(8)

WAR DIARY
or
INTELLIGENCE SUMMARY.

(Erase heading not required.)

Army Form C. 2118.

D.A.D.O.S.
29th Division

Place	Date	Hour	Summary of Events and Information	Remarks and references to Appendices
	Aug			
Rouen	12		Rouen re local purchase & Fireextinguishers with A.D.O.M.S.	P
Rouen	13		Base Depôts & A.D.O.S. Missions	P
— " —	14		D.D.O.S. Reserve Army formations	P
— " —	15		DADOS 29th Division re 29th Divisional Artillery	P
— " —	16		DADOS Reserve Division re transport etc	P
— " —	17		Beaumont re Ord Store Office	P
— " —	18		Removed Ord Store Office to Beaumont 29th Divisional Artillery reported to 6th Div & 7th Division Artillery attached same	P
			Tomorrow to Rouen for B.E.F.	
Beaumont	19		To Rear Headquarters to fetch Tours Tours for B.E.F.	P
— " —	20		ADOS 14th Corps re Bowls, Soche	P. P
— " —	21		Licence to Motoring Ford Store Officer	P
Treves	22		DADOS 29th Division re taking over his stores	P

Army Form C. 2118.

DADOS
20th Division

WAR DIARY
or
INTELLIGENCE SUMMARY.
(Erase heading not required.)

Instructions regarding War Diaries and Intelligence Summaries are contained in F. S. Regs., Part II. and the Staff Manual respectively. Title pages will be prepared in manuscript.

Place	Date	Hour	Summary of Events and Information	Remarks and references to Appendices
Scamps	23rd		Removed office staff to Albert Etablone (Sumais disliver)	
Albert Etablone	24th		To Amiens to purchase urge white figures for Gen. Staff	(1)
—	25th		To ADOS 14 Corps Meaulte & 61st Brigade HQ to front trenches	(2)
—	26th		Divisional Supply column near Corbie as nones	(2)
—	27th		Amiens re purchase of trench mirrors & holes, 3rd Australian Div. Sct.Sch.	(3)
—	28th		To OC Corps Troops re 500 shelter	(4)
—	29th		Amiens re bread puncheons. Armoured 6 mfg made 6000 reacher.	(5)
—	30th		To IOM Montmeant re running out springs	(6)
—	31st		To ADOS 14 Corps. 200 stretchers issued from Base. German made a gas attack. Sent blankets & anti-gas helmets up to front line	(7)

R.H. [signature] Capt.
DADOS 31/5/16
20th Division

Army Form C. 2118.

WAR DIARY
or
INTELLIGENCE SUMMARY.
(Erase heading not required.)

D.A.D.O.S
2nd Division Vol 11

Place	Date	Hour	Summary of Events and Information	Remarks and references to Appendices
Gezoncourt	Sept 1st		To Amiens to purchase numerous stores for G. Staff + performing numerous	(A)
"	2nd		To Abbeville to H.Q.B's Division. Conf. with senior members of Staff	(B)
"	3rd		To S.O.M. Maltencourt + DADOS 4th army	(C)
"	4th		To Amiens + Corbie re local purchases. 2nd Division etc	(D)
"	5th		Guillemont	(E)
"	6th		Corbie to fix up near Hdqtrs	(F)
"	7th		To D.H.Q. 14th Corps	(G)
Corbie	8th		Corbie New Site + Offices from 56th Division	(H)
"	9th		Letters out all Brigades with new instructions	(I)
"	10th		To General Supply Column re otto changes of H.Q. attend to institution of Divisions from 10th + Division between now + June 16	(J)
"	10th		To Siscount Distance to fix up for new units	(K)
"	10th		Hdqs at Corbie	
"	11th		To Amiens to purchase numerous stores for G. Staff	(L)

WAR DIARY or INTELLIGENCE SUMMARY

Army Form C. 2118.

Instructions regarding War Diaries and Intelligence Summaries are contained in F. S. Regs., Part II. and the Staff Manual respectively. Title pages will be prepared in manuscript.

(Erase heading not required.)

D.A.D.O.S
20th Division

Place	Date	Hour	Summary of Events and Information	Remarks and references to Appendices
Invenu Winter	12		Annual Stock Office to Inspect Mobile Stores. 13 men sick	(1)
			Machine Guns to Unit to replace lost	
"	13		To Corps re local purchase	(2)
"	14		To Ordnance A.D. Minden Post & Rue Faidherbe Estaizes	(3)
"	15		To A.D.O.S 14th Corps	(4)
"	16		To Armiens re local purchase. 20th Divn Artly reserve from Corps	(5)
"	17		Large numbers of Smoke Helmets from Base to replace unsatisfactory	(6)
			ones for 20th Divn I.A. also cancelling Indents & substitutes	
"	18		To Hqrs 20th Divn I.A. re Equipment	(7)
			Now for special Gun parts	
"	19		12 O.Rs attached to our Section orders to proceed at once to days	(8)
"	20		To A.D.O.S 14th Corps	(9)
"	21		To I.G.M. Rouen re ammunition. Division moved out of front line	(10)
			Enough 6th Divn	

WAR DIARY
or
INTELLIGENCE SUMMARY.
(Erase heading not required.)

Army Form C. 2118.

DA.D.O.S
20th Division

Place	Date	Hour	Summary of Events and Information	Remarks and references to Appendices
Tournai/Ath	22	—	Removed this office (part of) to Tournai. Suffyny 59 & 61st Brigades & D.H.Q. taken from this office & sent to Brigades from store at Tournai	®
Tournai	23	—	To A.D.O.S. 59th Division unit 458 Bridle Manger. Lining. Gum with subrooting from 59 & Brigade Hours	®
—	24	—	To Ammn re local purchases for G.Staff	®
—	25	—	To A.D.O.S. 14th Corps re Lewis Gun column	®
—	26	—	To 5th Division Brigade Transport Lines re Lewis Magazines & 59th Brigade H.Q.'s also 61st Brigade H.Q.'s with spare buckets	®
—	27	—	Removed Sub Office part to Tournai re Practice Ammn A.D.O.S. 14th Corps & S.O.M. Movements	® ®
—	28	—	Re. A.D.O.S. 14 Corps & 6.6 Stations Bowers re Lost Helmets	® ®
—	29	—	To Ammn re local purchases	®
—	30	—	To Ammn re local purchases & B.O. Corps Lorry Manifest	®

W.K.Brown Capt
D.A.D.O.S
20th Division 30/9/18

Vol 12

D.A.DOS
October 1946

Army Form C. 2118.

WAR DIARY
or
INTELLIGENCE SUMMARY

(Erase heading not required.)

D.A.D.O.S
20th Division

Place	Date Hour	Summary of Events and Information	Remarks and references to Appendices
Front	1st	To L.O.M. Movement & Missing Equipment re Lorries School of Instruction	A
"	2nd	To Advanced H.Q's Boundary Road re Boot Repairs	B
"	3rd	To Army Ordnance workshops re preparation of lorry Drivers note course next Monday	C
"		Men entered by 12 A.D	
"	4th	To A.D.O.S 1st Corps re Box Repairs	D
"	5th	Wrote re local purchase & to Divisions D.A.D.O.S	E
"	6th	To A.D.O.S 4th Corps re H.O.D Rifle wire cutters urgently required	F
"		by his Battalions in the line	
"	7th	To L.O.M. Winnetz re Ammunition carriers	G
"	8th	To Corps Salvage Officer re Steel helmets	H
"	9th	To Ammn re Local purchase Canvas Kit Bags 59 etc	I
		To Brigade Office & Ammn to France	

Army Form C. 2118.

D.A.D.O.S
20th Division

WAR DIARY
or
INTELLIGENCE SUMMARY.
(Erase heading not required.)

Place	Date	Hour	Summary of Events and Information	Remarks and references to Appendices
France	10th		To Treoins. Part of Store & Armr. returning at this Place to cover Div. Artillery, 20 & 21st Brigades &c. after further Rung a Feme.	
- " -	11th		To A.D.O.S 14th Corps re Ordnance (6th Division D+DOS)	
- " -	12th		To I.O Ar Mamch re Divisional Supply Column Lorrie	
- " -	13th		To Lorrie re finishing new State 1 Office	
Flortune	14th		Removed Stove 1 Office to Lorrie, leaving Ammunition Shop, & one M.O with small party of store at Treport to continue Arty re-ammunition from the true	
- " -	15th		Ar DADOS 7th Division Erindre to collect Ammre	
- " -	16th		To Armourers Shops & Store Treport	

WAR DIARY
or
INTELLIGENCE SUMMARY.
(Erase heading not required.)

Army Form C. 2118.

W.A.D.O.I
20th Division

Place	Date	Hour	Summary of Events and Information	Remarks and references to Appendices
Corbie	17		To A.D.O.S. 14th Corps & Docks & Field Ambces. Meaulte. Headqrs changed from Edgehill to Corbie	(A)
—	18		To 07.00 to 8th Division. Saw on transferring Artillery, & this units to Hem. Left 11.0.Z for observation cost of & Somme	(B)
—	19		Moved HQrs & Office from Sorcain & Corbie to Tignemont	(B) (C)
—	20		To Corbie. Saw Somme & find from Hem Fire & Office	(C)
Tignemont	20		Removed HQrs & Office to Belloy sur Somme. Saw 2 Hundred from Down Mayors the regiment to Infantry Brigades	(B)
—	21st		To A.D.O.2 10th Corps bridge.	(B)
Belloy Somme	22nd		To A.D.O.M. Albertville re inspecting as to Division Transport	(B)
—	23rd		To 60th Brigade H.Q. Schroeder, & see Northern Regiment.	(B)
—	24th		To 59th Brigade & all Units in Bussington with S.O.M. inspecting & her Transport	(B)
—	25th		To 61st Division 61st & 60th & 19th Brigades Transport. S.O.M. reports that the Division is far and away the best he has seen regarding the good woven and service in	(B)
—	26th		S.O.M. morning Transport.	(B)
—	27th		Forwarded to England on leave	B Williams GVS O 20th Division

Army Form C. 2118.

WAR DIARY
or
INTELLIGENCE SUMMARY.
(Erase heading not required.)

DAPPS
20th Division
Vol 13

Place	Date	Hour	Summary of Events and Information	Remarks and references to Appendices
Oroy	Nov 8th		Returned from leave & assumed Office rotten at Reserve to Army from Bolley sur Somme	
"	9th		To Amiens re boot purchase & other stamps	(?)
"	10th	9.0 am	Attended re repairs to Transport, told that mortars in car to have strike put a collar also harness, Board of Enquiry made then	(?)
"	11th		To Advance Brigade HQ's re stores transport. Lorries onto letters with 4 travelling kitchens to repair	(?) (?)
"	12th		Greater part of morning clothing issue	(?)
"	13th		To Amiens re purchase of small rollers for the Roads	(?) (?)
"	14th	9.0 am	Attended to fit Travel Counters	(?)
"	15th		Progress Office & store to Corbie	(?)
"	16th	9.0 am	Attended re making & issuing of issued cotton from Ordnance	R
"	17th		To Amiens re purchase of cubic centre for acetylene	(?)

Army Form C. 2118.

WAR DIARY
or
INTELLIGENCE SUMMARY.

D.A.D.O.S
20th Division

(Erase heading not required.)

Instructions regarding War Diaries and Intelligence Summaries are contained in F. S. Regs., Part II. and the Staff Manual respectively. Title pages will be prepared in manuscript.

Place	Date	Hour	Summary of Events and Information	Remarks and references to Appendices
Poix				
Contre	18th		To Pont Noyelle leaving school with Ecoyeur office	(1)
-"-	19th		To A.D.O.S 14th Corps (Mericourt) & Field Cashier. In Truck	(2)
-"-	20th		To Photo review	
-"-	21st		DADOS to 4th Army	(3)
-"-	22nd		To Albert re Funeral. Montiers to be repaired. 20M	(4)
-"-	23rd		To Amiens re making of a special G of Adm note	(5)
-"-	23rd		59th Brigade HQ % Title our Amiens re Blankets	(6)
-"-	24th		Lorries about Pont Noyelle & DADOS Guerrieu	(7)
-"-	25th		to ADOS 14 th Corps re transferring 91 st Brigade onwards	(8)
-"-	25th		from 29 re Div. to 4th Army Rew	
-"-	26th		Fred Cashier 14th Corps	(8)
-"-	27th		Corners re purchase of Acceptance reform for 5 Staff	(9)

1577 Wt. W10791/1773 500,000 1/15 D. D. & L. A.D.S.S./Forms/C. 2118.

Army Form C. 2118.

WAR DIARY
or
INTELLIGENCE SUMMARY.

(Erase heading not required.)

D.A.D.O.S. 20th Division

Place	Date	Hour	Summary of Events and Information	Remarks and references to Appendices
Orbie	26th		To D.D.O.S. 4th Army re the working of Wilson's Fire-lighters	(20)
" "	29th		To O.C. Salvage, 60th & 59th Brigade H'Quarters.	(21)
" "	30th		To Amiens re local purchase of Various stores & Motor Cycle Portmanteau	(22)

D. Brown Capt
D.A.D.O.S.
20th Division
29/1/16

1577 Wt. W10791/1773 500,000 1/15 D. D. & L. A.D.S.S./Forms/C. 2118.

WAR DIARY
or
INTELLIGENCE SUMMARY
(Erase heading not required.)

Army Form C. 2118

DADOS 20D
JJC 14

Place	Date	Hour	Summary of Events and Information	Remarks and references to Appendices
CORBIE	7.12.16	4 pm	Lieut. J. McGown A.O.D. arrived took over duty as temporary DADOS. during absence of Lt Col Browne	Mgg.
"	8.12.16		Visited ADOS XIV Corps and DADOS 29th Div re taking over.	Mgg.
"	9.12.16		Visited CRE. & ADMS. rent to Amiens for L.P.	Mgg.
"	10.12.16		Visited ADOS XIV Corps and 3rd Ordnance Mob Workshop.	Mgg.
"	11.12.16		Amiens on L.P. and 29th Div at #11.C.S.4.	Mgg.
#11.C.S.4	12.12.16		Moved to #11.C.S.4.	Mgg.
"	13.12.16		Visited railhead, both D.W.O.s (advanced & rear) searched pit site for little dumps.	Mgg.
"	14.12.16		Attended conference at ADOS XIV Corps etc.	Mgg.
"	15.12.16		Visited C in C, A.D.A., CRE. etc.	Mgg.
"	16.12.16		"O.O." Enroute. Amiens on L.P.	Mgg.
"	17.12.16		" All during stores in Division	Mgg.
"	18.12.16		" All staff Bde H.Q.s.	Mgg.
"	19.12.16		ADOS XIV Corps rewrite to him large dumps, for our nest divisional rest	Mgg.
"	20.12.16		Amiens on L.P. ADDOS at Camp.	Mgg.
"	21.12.16		ADOS XIV Corps.	Mgg.
"	22.12.16		Lt Col re taking over from 11th Div	Mgg.
"	23.12.16		Various units in Division, searched for a suitable dump for next period in Bois.	Mgg.
"	24.12.16		Routine	Mgg.
CORBIE	26.12.16		Moved to Corbie	Mgg.
"	26.12.16		Inspected vehicles for which reqs were demanded, refused to indent vehicles quite serviceable	Mgg.
"	27.12.16		Visited Amiens on L.P.	Mgg.
"	28.12.16		Routine	Mgg.
"	29.12.16		Visited ADOS XIV Corps, attended conference at D.H.Q. Submitted scheme for internment of ammunition short.	Mgg.
"	30.12.16		Visited Baths, various.	Mgg.
"	31.12.16		Visited Wharton, Bois. DADOS Ordnance re taking over.	Mgg.

Army Form C. 2118

WAR DIARY
or
INTELLIGENCE SUMMARY

(Erase heading not required.)

Vol 15

Confidential

War Diary
of
Capt. O. C. Thomas D.A.D.S. XX Division

From Jany 1st 1917 To. Jany 31st 1917

Army Form C. 2118

WAR DIARY
or
INTELLIGENCE SUMMARY
(Erase heading not required.)

Instructions regarding War Diaries and Intelligence Summaries are contained in F. S. Regs., Part II. and the Staff Manual respectively. Title Pages will be prepared in manuscript.

Place	Date	Hour	Summary of Events and Information	Remarks and references to Appendices
CORBIE	1-1-17		Visits [illegible] all men to prepare new dump. Visits Amiens on L.P. ffg.	
"	2 "		" Guillemin no Boots Guns. Maricourt. 17th Div. Ord. CBoS XIV Corps. Guards Ord. ffg.	
"	3 "		Moved ffg.	
"	4 "		Visits Corbie re Boots Guns. Various Wks. ffg.	
"	5 "		Went to Amiens through Capt.-Britons lect. ffg.	
"	6 "		Went on duties from [illegible] McEwan CD	
MARICOURT	7 "		" C.R.O.S. 17th Div Bgs. CD	
"	8 "		" S.O.M. re naming trough pit stand foll members CD	
"	9 "		" 60th Brigade H.Q. re arranging for 100 men to report to Ammun Dump everyday from Monto discharge this offer for one [illegible] removed by Divisional Engineers	
"	10 "		" 2000 ammn boxes on Div Amments kept.	
"	11 "		" Div. Water H.Q.o re sending lorries to S.A.M. to receive on making troughs CD	
"	12 "		" ADOS 14th Div. Bath. CD	
"	13 "		" OC Baths & Corbie L.P. CD	
"	14 "		" SOM Mamets CD	

Army Form C. 2118

WAR DIARY
or
INTELLIGENCE SUMMARY

(Erase heading not required.)

Instructions regarding War Diaries and Intelligence Summaries are contained in F. S. Regs., Part II. and the Staff Manual respectively. Title Pages will be prepared in manuscript.

Place	Date	Hour	Summary of Events and Information	Remarks and references to Appendices

[Handwritten entries illegible at this resolution]

Army Form C. 2118

WAR DIARY
or
INTELLIGENCE SUMMARY
(Erase heading not required.)

DADVS
XX Division

Place	Date	Hour	Summary of Events and Information	Remarks and references to Appendices
Méaulte	28th		Removed this office to Heilly	
Heilly	29th		No orders received. Routine	
"	30th		Sgt. A.D.V.S. to the Corps	
"	31st		Remains in bad quarters	

D.B. Brown Capt
D.A.D.V.S.
23rd Division

WO/16

CONFIDENTIAL

WAR DIARY
of
D.A.D.O.S. 20th Divn

FEBRUARY. 1917

WAR DIARY or INTELLIGENCE SUMMARY

Army Form C. 2118

Place	Date	Hour	Summary of Events and Information	Remarks and references to Appendices
MARICOURT BOIS.	8-2-17		Moved from Meilly. Capt Evans orders to report to XIV Corps for temporary duty.	Pg 99.
"	9-2-17		Evans new duty. Erects officers. Evans took up duty etc.	Pg 99.
"	10-2-17		Inspected all wagons of D.A.C. Found most of them in very bad condition remains with I.O.M. to then refair or overhauled.	Pg 99.
"	11-2-17		Inspected all Gun limbers during work clothes on a period of Spinks.	Pg 99.
"	12-2-17		Attended conference at XIV Corps re Gun limbers, clothes retraining of Spinks.	Pg 99.
"	13-2-17		Visited Gunners on L.P.	Pg 99.
"	14-2-17		Visited 18 Pdr W.5 Gun in action to see use of certain ordnance supplies	Pg 99.
"	15-2-17		Gunners in L.P. for XIV Corps.	Pg 99.
"	16-2-17		" 60 pdrs 16th Army H.A.	Pg 99.
"	17-2-17		" G.O.C. Division, Divnl Dirs	Pg 99.
"	18-2-17		Routine.	Pg 99.
"	19-2-17		Visited all salvage dumps. d.O.M.	Pg 99.
"	20-2-17		" Gunners on L.P. for XIV Corps.	Pg 99.
"	21-2-17		" XIV Corps Lt. Army H.A.	Pg 99.
"	22-2-17		" Front line trenches to see condition under which clothing Guns took over was	Pg 99.
"	23-2-17		Guns took during Diss 59th 16th Bde H.A.S.	Pg 99.
"	24-2-17		Routine.	Pg 99.
"	25-2-17		Betting in action.	Pg 99.
"	26-2-17		Gunners th L.P. I XIV Corps.	Pg 99.
"	27-2-17		XIV Corps.	Pg 99.
"	28-2-17		Capt. Evans left the division. Proceeded direct from late to base Boulogne.	Pg 99.

28·2·17 [signature] Capt.
D.A.D.O.S. 2 Div.
20·2·17

Vol. 17

WAR DIARY
OF
D.A.D.O.S. 20th Division

MARCH 1917

Army Form C. 2118

WAR DIARY
or
INTELLIGENCE SUMMARY
(Erase heading not required.)

Instructions regarding War Diaries and Intelligence Summaries are contained in F. S. Regs., Part II. and the Staff Manual respectively. Title Pages will be prepared in manuscript.

Place	Date	Hour	Summary of Events and Information	Remarks and references to Appendices
MARICOURT BOIS	1-3-17		Routine /98.	
"	2-3-17		Visited XIV Corps /98.	
"	3-3-17		" Train Conference held D.A.C. /98.	
"	4-3-17		Routine /98.	
"	5-3-17		Visits various units re question of improvised packsaddlery /98.	
"	6-3-17		" Review in L.P. /98.	
"	7 -		Routine /98. Horse Show /98.	
"	8 -		Visited XIV Corps. Review in L.P. /98.	
"	9 -		Routine. Paytos M.S.Vet D.A.C. 159 Coys. Vet /98.	
"	10 -		Attended Anti-Divisional Conference. Inspects Transport wagons /98.	
MARICOURT	11 -		Inspects Gun Limbers. D.A.C. wagons. Visits Salvage Dump Central /98. /98.	
"	12 -		Visits Exchange Dump advanced D.A.C. &c. /98.	
"	13 -		" Review in L.P. /98.	
"	14 -		Routine /98.	
"	15 -		Attended Conference at Reviews /98.	
"	16 -		Visits to Army re improvised packsaddlery /98.	
"	18 -		" all forward area. D.A.C.	
"	19 -		Routine /98.	
"	20 -		Visits C.R.S. &c &c /98.	
"	21 -		Visits Review in L.P. /98.	
"	22 -		" New horse lines situation inspected by Cavalry. Very little labour left, ground seems to me have been carefully cleaned, much better than our last visit /98.	
"	23 -		Routine /98.	

Army Form C. 2118

WAR DIARY
or
INTELLIGENCE SUMMARY
(Erase heading not required.)

Instructions regarding War Diaries and Intelligence Summaries are contained in F.S. Regs., Part II. and the Staff Manual respectively. Title Pages will be prepared in manuscript.

Place	Date	Hour	Summary of Events and Information	Remarks and references to Appendices
MARICOURT	24-3-17		Visits A.D.O.S. HQr.	
"	25 "		Changes from XIV to XV Corps.	
"	26 "		Visits A.D's XIV XV Corps HQr.	
"	27 "		Routine. D.D.O.S. Lt Conroy Bethelis Dump. HQr.	
"	28 "		Visits Engineers on L.P. HQr	
"	29 "		Routine. HQr.	
"	30 "		Visits Amiens on L.P. HQr	
"	31 "		Routine. A.D.O.S. XV bd. inspects Dump. HQr.	

Always available - the train, but mostly R.S. HQr.
visits Peronne, R.S. always available - the train, but mostly R.S. HQr.

[signature] Lieut.
D.A.D.O.S. 2.D. Div.
31-3-17.

Army Form C. 2118

WAR DIARY
or
INTELLIGENCE SUMMARY
(Erase heading not required.)

DADOS 20 D
Oct 18

Place	Date	Hour	Summary of Events and Information	Remarks and references to Appendices
Maricourt	1 & 2		Visited 2" Army Workshop	
	3 & 4		D.H.Q. moved to Rocquigny, whilst Mess Stores, Canvas & Horse dump, for want of railroads	
	5		held Salvage dump is in old area	
	6			
	7			
	8		As D.H.Q. is 11 miles away & on the road is not fit for motor	
	9		cars, I take all day to visit them	
	10			
	11			
	12		Went on leave for 14 days	
	13			
Rocquigny	26		Went to Rocquigny	
	30		Returned from leave	

Certified true copy

[signature] Capt.
DADOS 20 Div.

1875 Wt. W593/826 1,000,000 4/15 J.B.C. & A. A.D.S.S./Forms/C. 2118.

Instructions regarding War Diaries and Intelligence Summaries are contained in F. S. Regs., Part II. and the Staff Manual respectively. Title Pages will be prepared in manuscript.

War Diary Vol 19

D.A.D.O.S

Gray 1917

WAR DIARY or INTELLIGENCE SUMMARY

Army Form C. 2118

Place	Date	Hour	Summary of Events and Information	Remarks and references to Appendices
ROCQUIGNY	1-5-19		Routine.	
"	2 "		New drafts joined at Rocquigny there being no lack of instructions how to do everything, work satisfactorily rapidly. There was, as usual, no ramp, but none was required today.	
"	3 "		Orders today received that no men were to be killed over Xmas. I last move all my men. I found there was plenty of material left by Bosch to build up the necessary huts.	
"	4 "		Which had to be sent back to transcent Bois, owing to want of work at Rocquigny	
"	5 "		On night of 3rd. the inst. Gas alarms sounded. All my men rally were in Rocquigny acted promptly quickly. One Labour Batn in Area, attached to left, had no helmets. Rocquigny has to supply to my dump for them after alarm has sounded on 3rd visit. They also sent for a further 60 for draft. after the two bungers or it appears that more careful inspection shows he made of gas incidents in isolated units.	
"	6/7 "		Inspections were of 180 Mr Train Coys all is fairly good but require painting etc	
"	8 "		Visited Sudicourt L.P. Car took us down on return journey, had it to double wheel that it was refused twelve refugees in about 2 hours, it would have meant at least a week for them.	
"	9 "		Force inst truly in need of paint, of which supply is being demanded at Base. As this is the time of year when all weapon stores is bitterly needed to ameliorate any scarcity of paint at Base. Special arrangements shares to made to obviate any scarcity of paint at Base.	

WAR DIARY
or
INTELLIGENCE SUMMARY

Army Form C. 2118

Place	Date	Hour	Summary of Events and Information	Remarks and references to Appendices
ROEUX	10-5-17		Severe out harness lists, does not show a shortage of wheels Nos 200 and this there are 138 due to this formation. I took the matter up with C in C today. fb.	
"	11-5-17		Woolwich Col. orders d/6-5-17 received it is suggested that the provision is not sent to Divisional Ordnance, as if so they would deal with provision of A.O.C. at bases we per items dealt with by officers in the danger zone, a personal attached to Division hence difficulties fg.	
"	12-5-17		Visits cannons in L.P. fg.	
"	13-5-17		Inspects vehicles of 113 Sec D.A.C. there is a marked improvement in the manner in which they are kept. fg.	
"	14-5-17		Instructs Flynn vehicles. Paint lorries colour to wheels No 200, are very badly needed but I cannot get either from here. fg.	
"	16-5-17			
"	17-5-17		Series complaint about oil to fulfilling from R.A. The oil is very thin slight. cud for complaint in writing to forward to Corps. fg.	
"	19-5-17		Visits Cannons on L.P. visits A.D.O.S. XV Corps fg.	
"	20-5-17		Wild shoots for detachment car. Sir visits Roeux gun fg. Instructs Sec 1+2 D.A.C. Weypro all good but badly in need of paintwheels fg.	
"	21/22 & 23		Visits I.O.M. N° 20 XV Corps. Luffers oil refills very bad. G.S.f to fg. writing. hands bunt to W.I.B. @ G.S. fg.	

WAR DIARY or INTELLIGENCE SUMMARY

Army Form C. 2118

Place	Date	Hour	Summary of Events and Information	Remarks and references to Appendices
Hd. Qrs. near FARBUS	24.5.17 25/5/17		Forward new dump fixed. Visited A.D.S. LDDOS fig. Visited various units. There is little or great outcry for No 200 wheels. Paid particular attention to ADS's about it. Pointed out that up to the whole, that they do fairly well in replacing that in spite of this there is very often a great shortage. I think the question of wheel retain stops in Army Area should be considered. fig. Visited D.A.D.O.S. LDDOS fig. Requiring replaced to see that all our returned stores had been sent off. correctly fig. Visited batteries in camouflage. At last for this unit without much difficulty fig. Went to Aimiens L.P. fig. Being thorough I drew attention to forthcoming Order 174 of 3-4-17. Q MG 10/31 (6 B2) 28-3-17. No Rifles for rifle grenade, I pointed out to Army (through Corps) that the grenade practically amounted to a new rifle for each round of stick grenade. I was told to carry out this order, so have asked DADOS to issue the necessary instructions fig.	
"	28 "			
"	29/5/30			
"	31 "			

21-5-17

H. Lyon. Capt.
D.A.D.O.S. 20 Div.

WAR DIARY OF D.A.D.O.S 20th Divn

JUNE 1917

Vol 20

Q 20184/12

WAR DIARY
or
INTELLIGENCE SUMMARY

Army Form C. 2118.

Place	Date	Hour	Summary of Events and Information	Remarks and references to Appendices
ZARREN WIL	1-6-17		Visits to OrO, ORP, Troops & Light Ordnance Workshops.	A/98
"	2/3 "		Still experience great difficulty in obtaining Wule No. 200. Service Ledgers just the want of paint cards, & pages in Imperial Pay account of Imprest charge of train. Introduced a new system by which all Laundry Pieces are Stencilled which has shown much duplication & identical issues returned open Underwear in they Bris.	A/98
"	4-6-17		Visited Ordnance re (1st part of the) Ordnance Administration.	A/98
"	5-6-17		Visited Amiens re L.P.	A/98
"	6/7 "		Inspected Br. train Havre — it is well kept.	A/99
"	8 "		Went to Army Gun Park, driving to Gun show.	A/98
"	9/10 "		Experienced great difficulty in obtaining Guns 18hr 14.5Hors Guns late. 5th Army Gun Park say they have no Guns or Stores Registers though about who replies to Section Gun Pak. Went & kept got no satisfaction Went to DOOS. It has not yet Arrived Gun Park. Light Gun kept not show but got finds. Got some late on 10th.	A/98
"	11 "		in area. Left message for him. Heavy rain on night of 10th morning of 11th came through stove rest hut & brought kegwood (recently issued with line of cutts) with it. Some clothing stacks & stove destroyed. Notified Base DOOS by wire.	A/98
"	12 "		Visits A97 in action.	A/98
"	13 "		Inspected Hanveo of 160 Coy A.S.C. & 7th Divisnal C.S.	A/98
"	14 "		Visits I.O.M. Depo 24 & 29. Hy Camp was inspected by A.D.O.S. II Corps.	A/98

A5834 Wt. W4973/M687 750,000 8/16 D. D. & L. Ltd. Forms/C.2118/13.

Army Form C. 2118.

WAR DIARY
or
INTELLIGENCE SUMMARY.
(Erase heading not required.)

Instructions regarding War Diaries and Intelligence Summaries are contained in F.S. Regs., Part II. and the Staff Manual respectively. Title pages will be prepared in manuscript.

Place	Date	Hour	Summary of Events and Information	Remarks and references to Appendices
JAVREUIL	15-6-17		Inspected Rifles, Pistols, Lewis Guns of 7th K.O.Y.L.I. Bde.	
"	16 "		Visited Gun Park, Inspected Workshop Bde.	
"	17 "		Inspected Rifles, Pistols, Lewis Guns of 7th D.C.L.I. Bde.	
"	18 "		" " " " 7th Somersets C.I. Bde.	
"	19 "		" " " " 12th King's Liverpools Bde.	
"	20 "		Visited I.O.M. 24 Workshop. Inspected Lewis Guns of 8th Devons Bde.	
"	21 "		A.D.O.S. re Paint Bde.	
"	22 "		Gunpark re guns Cannot yet any 1817 14 5-4 bren Bde.	
"	23 "		Chief le grand re Lewis Guns Bde.	
"	24 "		Corbiere at Heaute Storie out Bde.	
"	25 "		Beauville re Lewis Guns Bde.	
"	26 "		Routine Bde.	
"	27 "		Owing to large dumps of unfired ammunition of lumens lying about with 1st Division has really all sand, but metal worn through Bde.	
BERNAVILLE	28 "		Moved to Beauville Bde.	
"	29 "		Under Hostel numbers. Visited Chloroelle on L.P. Bde.	
"	30 "		Routine Bde.	

Osborn Capt.
D.A.D.O.S. 20. Div.

YC 21

War Diary
000000
July 1917

WAR DIARY or INTELLIGENCE SUMMARY

Army Form C. 2118.

Place	Date	Hour	Summary of Events and Information	Remarks and references to Appendices
BERNAFAY	1-7-17		Visits Genl Pat at Allot, & Artillery at Trecourt Wg.	
"	2 "		" Aberdeen L.P., 59th Bn., 59th M.G. Coy. Wg.	
"	3 "		Inspects vehicles of 12th Kings Rfg.	
"	4 "		Inspected S.A.A. Guns of 59th M.G. Coy. & Ammn on L.P. Wg.	
"	5 "		" 16 " " 60th M.G. Coy.	
"	6 "		" 8 " " 217. " Lewis Guns of 7th Somerset. Wg.	
"	6 "		" 8 " " 217.	
"	7 "		" 8 " " 8 of 61st M.G. Coy. Wg.	
"	8 "		" 8 " 61st M.G. Coy. Suggests to Div that Lewis Gunners should only be	
"			condemned by Q.M.s direct by bny Commanders Wg.	
"	9 "		Visits Gunners on L.P. Wg.	
"	10 "		Attends G.O.C. inspection 11th K.R.R. Finds no effort appears to be made to repair small holes in	
"			tunics, back etc. Recommends that these attention be given to repair	
"	11 "		Inspects, when necessary repaired, all small arms & ammn of 10th K.R.R. Wg.	
"	12 "		" " 12th K.R.R. & 6th K.S.L.I. Wg.	
"	13 "		" " 12th R.B. & 6th K.S.L.I. Wg.	
"	14 "		" " 7th D.C.L.I. & 7th K.O.Y.L.I. Wg.	
"	15 "		" " 14th D.C.L.I. & 12th Kings Wg.	
"	16 "		At Observation. All Arms were found to be well looked after except 7th K.O.Y.L.I. Wg.	
"			" 11th R.B.	
"			" 10th R.B. & 11th R.B. Wg.	
"	17		Insp'd J.O.M. rounds & small arms & infantry vehicles. Wg.	

WAR DIARY
or
INTELLIGENCE SUMMARY.

Army Form C.2118

Instructions regarding War Diaries and Intelligence Summaries are contained in F.S. Regs., Part II. and the Staff Manual respectively. Title pages will be prepared in manuscript.

(Erase heading not required.)

Place	Date	Hour	Summary of Events and Information	Remarks and references to Appendices
BERNAVILLE	18-7-17		Routine.	
"	19-7-17		Went to PROVEN arrange for erection of new camp. Visited Artillery HQ.	
"	16/19-7-17		Call mats late Kitchen travelling were repaired or new issued by I.O.M. new Kitchens three dates.	
"	19-7-17		A further inspection of 11th K.R.R. ammo was made, ammo now satisfactory. HQ	
"	20-7-17		Visited I.O.M. Abbeville.	
"	21-7-17		Moved to Proven. HQ	
PROVEN			Visited CRDOS x10 Corps + O.O.C.T. HQ	
"	22 "		" Calais Base. Cannot get Latho. HQ	
"	23 "		" ADOS DOS. I.O.M. Guns necessary for Artillery were not supplied whilst Gatling was connected, Cd. hook had necessary stepo to obtain HQ	
"	24 "		Went to Calais Base, to draw ammunition or available. pps	
"	25 "		Visited CRDOS, HQ Coy, I.O.M. Gun Park. Received 16,509 extensions L.B. respirators entered almost 50% had lost its value in transit trying to less packing demanded to replace many units demanding Respirators, Coy of Balance of my attempt.	
"	26 "		Base. The scale of 1500 M Division does not appear to be sufficient, when So hew. are being used by Bdes. HQ	
"	27 "		Stells are being used by Bdes. HQ Visited 59 Bd HQ, found they dissatisfied with delay in supply of ammo Bench carts, hand grenade gun Parts to Supplying but were hampered by vehicles from the many later transport as Bomb must be replaced by new.	
"	28 "		On L.P. to Ecko HQ Visited both Rln Rdos. HQ	

Army Form C. 2118.

WAR DIARY
or
INTELLIGENCE SUMMARY.
(Erase heading not required.)

Instructions regarding War Diaries and Intelligence Summaries are contained in F. S. Regs., Part II. and the Staff Manual respectively. Title pages will be prepared in manuscript.

Place	Date	Hour	Summary of Events and Information	Remarks and references to Appendices
PROVEN	29.7.17		Visited 10th Bn. L.O.M. LLOYDS HQs.	
	30		" 60 - & GrenPal. HQs.	
	31		Went StOmer on L.P. visited ADDS HQs.	

Allen Colt 20 Div
B.A.D.O.S.
31-7-17

Vol 22

WAR DIARY
DADOS

DADOS

Army Form C. 2118.

WAR DIARY
or
INTELLIGENCE SUMMARY.
(Erase heading not required.)

Instructions regarding War Diaries and Intelligence Summaries are contained in F. S. Regs., Part II. and the Staff Manual respectively. Title pages will be prepared in manuscript.

Place	Date	Hour	Summary of Events and Information	Remarks and references to Appendices
PROVEN	1-8-17		Went Calais Base re stores /pg.	
"	2-8-17		Accordingly to his new dump, visits to R.A + hus 1 + 2 Bac. /pg.	
"	3-		few cases to find dump. Gun Park a.o.s. /pg.	
"	4-		Gun Park. Ordnance 58. D.s. /pg.	
"	5-		J.O.M. new camp /pg.	
"	6-		moves to new camp. Reports to ADOS XIV Corps that I could not comply with any new orders re reports positions etc. continue to carry on my late duties without clerical assistance. We have the same number of clerks as has in Aug 14, but keep four times the amount of office work. Gotroffes /pg.
Aq. D.S. 8 Sep 28			Visits Railhead. W/A Bse. 15t Rde. /pg.	
	7-		Herschoof or L.P. Gun Park. /pg.	
	8-		ADOS. J.O.M. Camp was inspected by ADOS /pg.	
	9-		St Georgen L.P. new Gun Park J.O.M. /pg.	
	10-		A.D.O.S. /pg.	
	11-		Calais Base re Canvases etc. /pg.	
	12-		J.O.M. Inspected Vannes of W. Field Amb. /pg.	
	13-		Gun Park. ADOS. Cannot get Provendal Conferees, delay in servising demau interference. Sent full report to Army through ADOS. /pg.	
	14			

Army Form C. 2118.

WAR DIARY
or
INTELLIGENCE SUMMARY.
(Erase heading not required.)

Instructions regarding War Diaries and Intelligence Summaries are contained in F. S. Regs. Part II. and the Staff Manual respectively. Title pages will be prepared in manuscript.

Place	Date	Hour	Summary of Events and Information	Remarks and references to Appendices
Aq. B.3-8 Sheet 28	15-8-17		Routine MSg.	
	16		Visited 6th Bn S.R. in line. Lines. Depaired to Lewis Webber Gung again & B.B. very heavy, but all demands so far late been met by Gun Pak without slightest delay. MSg.	
"	17		Draft was inspected by D.O.S. Zllt Army, visited Gun Park, L.O.M. MSg Etc. Prov. camp. Loves part of camp MSg.	
"	18			
"	19		In defence of roving M. Guns Lewis Gun inanous essential stores from a Gun Pk in fighting area. We prove very loved these of the created assistance to the Division MSg. Moves to Proven MSg.	
PROVEN	20		Built camp, went to 2nd Army Inchef MSg. moved army MSg.	
"	21		camp inspects by Soc. Inspects with sch Army 7th Corps, 7th S.L.I. + 12th Kings. The proportion of interruptions was more than what being 20%. This was mostly caused by the bad weather, the ground was very soft. Some rifle no doubt, were fired, whilst dirt was in the barrel. Bayonets do not appear to be good as formerly. 17% were unserviceable MSg.	
"	22		Inspected rifles & bayonets of 6.6.B. 6. K.S.L.I. 12 K.R.R. + 12 R.B. all kept mud, letting car formerly. Visited RA. MSg.	
"	23		Visited 159 + 160 Cooft Coy, all vehicles were kept MSg	
"	24		West Gun Pak, L.O.M. & B.Q. R.A. MSg.	

Army Form C. 2118.

WAR DIARY
or
INTELLIGENCE SUMMARY.
(Erase heading not required.)

Instructions regarding War Diaries and Intelligence Summaries are contained in F. S. Regs., Part II. and the Staff Manual respectively. Title pages will be prepared in manuscript.

Place	Date	Hour	Summary of Events and Information	Remarks and references to Appendices
PROVEN.	25.8.17		West Sandhill on L.P. HQs.	
"	26	"	Inspected 59th Bde Ammn. HQs.	
"	27	"	Inspected belg. T.M. B's. W.D.L.I. HQs.	
"	28	"	Visited Base Chaine & stores HQs.	
"	29	"	Inspected repairs at 59th Bde HQs.	
"	30	"	Visited A.D.O.S. XIV Corps HQs.	
"	31	"	61st Bde W.C HQs.	

During the week 19/31st all rifles, Lewis & Stokes guns were inspected. They show a great improvement in the care with which they are kept. The theft of bicycles amongst units has increased, & only to absorb this, all cycles are now being numbered & returns of any units found with a bicycle to which it is not entitled will have that bicycle confiscated. This is called upon to replace it at unit expense. The refitting of Divisions which are now being placed by very light overnight to all winter hutting up to seen during of section, so far as is possible HQ.

31-8-17

W. Glenn Coll.
O. C. A.P.O.S. 20th Dn

Vol 23

War Diary
DADOS
20th Divn
Sept 1917

Army Form C. 2118.

WAR DIARY
or
INTELLIGENCE SUMMARY.
(Erase heading not required.)

Instructions regarding War Diaries and Intelligence Summaries are contained in F. S. Regs., Part II. and the Staff Manual respectively. Title pages will be prepared in manuscript.

Place	Date	Hour	Summary of Events and Information	Remarks and references to Appendices
PROVEN	1-9-17		Visited Div. Arty. H.Q. Gun Pits. T.O.M. Pos.	
"	2-9-17		Went on leave 2/13 with MSS.	
"	10-9-17		Had to G/16 B Bdge. Pos.	
Arb B3-7	13-"-"		Returned off leave Pos.	
Shed 28	14 -		Visited Railheads. Div. H.A. D&C. Div. Arty. MSS.	
"	15 -		Inspected No.1 Sub.D.A.C. wagons etc. Pos.	
"	16		" 2 " " MSS.	
"	17		" 3 " " MSS.	
"	18		Inspected H.Q. Coy Div. trans. wagons, all very good. MSS.	
"	19		Visited Cdrs. Workshop. Pos.	
"	20		Visited Bde. H.Q. Batteries in action MSS.	
"	21		" " Div. Arty. Batteries in action MSS.	
"	22		" " Front MSS.	
"	23		" " A.D.O.S. & A.D.V.S MSS.	
"	24		Went to Dinner on L.P. MSS.	
"	25		Inspected DAC letters Leaving, all good MSS.	
"	26		Routine MSS.	
"	27		Visited A.D.O.S. A.D.V.S MSS.	
"	28		Went to new area Pos. MSS.	
ROCQUIGNY	29		Moved camp MSS.	
"	30			

WAR DIARY
or
INTELLIGENCE SUMMARY.

Army Form C. 2118.

Part 2
Vol 24

Place	Date	Hour	Summary of Events and Information	Remarks and references to Appendices
FINS	15.10.17		Returned from Ammunition course HQ.	
"	16		Visits D.D.O.S. 3rd Army HQ.	
"	17		A.D.O.S. VII Corps + D.A.D.O.S. Redeemed HQ	
"	18		Inspects transport of Kings HQ.	
"	19		Visits Armourer L.P. HQ.	
"	20		Revises armd vault Civilian HQ.	
"	21		Inspects harness workshop of Royals HQ.	
"	22		Inspected harness HQ ve D.L.C. HQ.	
"	23			
"	24		Attended Conf conference HQ.	
"	25		Pouders HQ.	
"	26		Inspects all rifles rods cups of S.A.A. HQ.	
"	27		Inspects lewis guns of R.S. Regt "	
"	28		With Armourer to L.P. "	
"	29		Inspects transport of Co. Recce HQ.	
NURLU	30		On arrival new camp visited Corp HQ	
"	31		Men sent to take HQ	
"			went to Sunr Park HQ.	

Major & Lt Col
D.A.D.O.S. 20. Div.

Army Form C. 2118.

D.A.D.o.S

VII 25

WAR DIARY
or
INTELLIGENCE SUMMARY.
(Erase heading not required.)

Instructions regarding War Diaries and Intelligence Summaries are contained in F.S. Regs., Part II. and the Staff Manual respectively. Title pages will be prepared in manuscript.

Place	Date	Hour	Summary of Events and Information	Remarks and references to Appendices
NURLU	1-11-19		Duties inspected by A.D.O.S /8s.	
	2		Review on L.P /8s.	
	3		Visited BG2 in line /8s.	
	4		Routine /8s.	
	5		Review on L.P /8s.	
	6		Look over Batt. clothing necessary /8s.	
	7		Inspected all Div Baths. Went Ent. laundry at Amas /8s.	
	8		Went to Gun Park /8s.	
	9		Visited Rate Book Café /8s.	
	10		" III & VII Cort Book /8s.	
	11		Routine /8s.	
	12		Visited III bury VII VI /8s.	
	13		" ADOS III Corps /8s.	
	14		" Gun Park /8s.	
	15		Went to Villers Plouich to find advanced dump /8s.	
	16		Visited ADS RE /8s.	
	17		Visited advanced gun park /8s.	
	18		Found new dump at Villers Plouich /8s.	
	19		Visited all Brigades returned etc. - /8s.	
	20			
	21			

WAR DIARY
or
INTELLIGENCE SUMMARY.

Army Form C. 2118.

Place	Date	Hour	Summary of Events and Information	Remarks and references to Appendices
NURLU	22-11-17		Visits Advanced dump and 59th Bde HQ	
	23		" " " 91st A By Bde HQ	
	24		" " " 61st Bde HQ	
	25		" " " 92nd A By Bde	went LauwPak
	26		" " " A92. B92 Cpn	
	27		" " " Gengecourt huts	
	28		Went Larmecourt P	
	29		" Advanced dump	
	30		Started, all ready to retreat	

WAR DIARY or INTELLIGENCE SUMMARY

Army Form C. 2118.

Place	Date	Hour	Summary of Events and Information	Remarks and references to Appendices
NURLU	1-12-17		Stand to style as usual.	
"	2		" off. visited VII Corps re clothing.	
"	3		Went to D.A.D.S. 5th Army.	
"	4		" Beaupreau to Peronne.	
"	5		Prepared for move.	
"	6		Visited C.D.O.S. moved to Hucqueliers.	
HUCQUEL- IERS	7		Went to Beaupreau to look for Adv. pty.	
"			moved to Blaringhem.	
BLARINGHEM	8		Went Hucqueliers to D.H.Q. etc x Adv pty.	
"	9		Routine	
"	10		Went 3rd Army Laundry Beauvais.	
"	11		Routine	
"	12		Visited 59 Heavy, 96 Field Coy.	
"	13		" A.D.O.S. & O.R.C.	
"	14		" 60th Rde.	
"	15		St Hand Gr. P.	
"	16		visited 59 Bde H.Q., 60th Bde H.Q. and 61st Wilsby.	
"	17		Inspected rifles of 12th K.R.R.C.	
"	18			
"	19			

Army Form C. 2118.

WAR DIARY
or
INTELLIGENCE SUMMARY.
(Erase heading not required.)

Place	Date	Hour	Summary of Events and Information	Remarks and references to Appendices
BLARINGHEM	20.12.17		Went to believe to follow there for Our Artillery conveys sent to prevent MG.	
	21 "		Unable to get to Review today. Inspected rifles at O.C. E.S. Hqrs.	
	22 "		Review MG. Inspected rifles of Range Wardrobes MG.	
	23 "		Inspected rifles of 11 RB + 12 KRRC. Visited 59, 60, 61st Bde M.O.s. MG.	
	24 "		Inspected arms of 10 RB & 11 KRR. visited 96 Fd Coy + 61st Fd A. MG.	
	25 "		Being Xmas Day had inspect of trucks. Routine MG.	
	26 "		Visited 59 Bde Bar MG.	
	27 "		Leaves Home to Our City en route MG.	
	28 "		Inspected arms of 60 Bde MG.	
	29 "		Went to Calais for lime MG.	
	30 "		Went to new Area in lorry over MG.	
	31 "		Attended G.O.C. inspection of 61 R.B. visit MG.	

B. Loor Cott
20" Div
D.A.D.O.S.
31-12-17

WAR DIARY or INTELLIGENCE SUMMARY

Army Form C. 2118.

DADOS / Vol 27

Place	Date	Hour	Summary of Events and Information	Remarks and references to Appendices
BLARINGHEM	1-1-18		Went to Wizernes re taking over [illeg]	
"	2 "		Inspected all Dishm Gangs of Div Ry.	
"	3 "		Visited Arty T.M.Bs. 160. Bde HQs	
"	4 "		" Divy & DDOS Lillers [illeg]	
"	5 "		Attended Conference HQs	
"	6 "		Moved to Westoutre [illeg]	
WEST OUTRE	7 "		Visited Baths at Vijverhoek & St Jans Cappel [illeg]	
"	8 "		" Chippewa, " O.i/c Div Lootlo[illeg] Brasserie [illeg]	
"	9 "		" - St Jans Cappel, Chippewa - Wing LADOS IX Corps [illeg]	
"	10 "		" to R.G Coy. Attended Conference of Staff Captains & HQ MG at Oblée [illeg]	
"	11 "		" Chippewa Baths, 59th Div HQs, Vijverhoek Baths, Brunhoek Stn, Brasserie, & Reninghelst [illeg]	
"	12 "		" I.W.G.R.R, IX R.R. " visits & D.D.C. [illeg]	
"	13 "		" Brunhoek Stores, Salvage Dump, Laundry [illeg]	
"	14 "		DADOS went on leave. Visited Green Boot Store & Vijverhoek baths with D.A.Q.M.G. RE [illeg]	
"	15 "		Visited Baths officer visited VIJVERHOEK Baths & St Jans CAPEL Laundry [illeg]	
"	16 "		" St JANS CAPEL Laundry.	
"	17 "		" St. JANS CAPEL LAUNDRY - 124th Bde R.F.A - ADOS IX Corps. Baths officer visited Chippewa Baths [illeg]	
"	18 "		Baths officer visited St JANS CAPEL, CHIPPEWA, & VIJVERHOEK baths. Chippewa & Vijverhoek baths [illeg]	
"	19 "		Visited St JANS CAPEL Laundry.	
"	20 "		" ADOS IX Corps, St Jans Capel Laundry - French Army authorities [illeg]	
"			Bifficulin Baths at WEST OUTRE & St JANS CAPEL Laundry.	
"			Routine Visits CHIPPEWA baths.	

Army Form C. 2118.

WAR DIARY
or
INTELLIGENCE SUMMARY.
(Erase heading not required.)

Place	Date	Hour	Summary of Events and Information	Remarks and references to Appendices
WESTOUTRE	21.1.18.		Visited VYVERHOEK, ST JANS CAPPEL Balls Laundry.	
"	22	"	St JANS CAPPEL Laundry	
"	23	"	Routine	
"	24	"	Visited 123rd Bde R.F.A. - Ordered visits VYVERHOEK, CHIPPEWA, huts.	
"	25	"	BLENDECQUES Laundry.	
"	26	"	St JANS CAPPEL, VYVERHOEK, CHIPPEWA	
"	27	"	Routine. Visited VYVERHOEK, etc.	
"	28	"	Visited VYVERHOEK.	
"	29	"	D.D.O.S. returns from leave	
"	30	"	Visited Lullaps Camp. Signed. transfer cert.	
"	31	"	D.S.C. & St Jans Cappel laundry	

Major Capt.
B. Abbot, 2nd Div
31-1-18.

WAR DIARY
or
INTELLIGENCE SUMMARY.

Army Form C. 2118.

STAND 8 202

Vol 28

Place	Date	Hour	Summary of Events and Information	Remarks and references to Appendices
WESTOUTRE	1-2-18		Visited Chilleurs Wynhoek & D.L.C. Yes.	
"	2	"	XII Corps A.D.O.S. and St Omer Cattle Yes.	
"	3	"	Wynhock, new fort exchange, Chilleurs Yes.	
"	4	"	31st Divl Cattle, Brewsteen new stands Bns	
"	5	"	D.O.S. North " " "	
"	6	"	A.D.O.S. XVII Corps. "	
"	7	"	Chilleurs Camps, "	
"	8	"	Wynhoek, new Rahn. Institute of huntness Yes	
"	9	"	A.C.C. 123, R.S.A. Ralteun Yes	
"	10	"	31st Div Cattle NQ Yes	
"	11	"	" " "	
"	12	"	10th. div to Battubul on L.P. Yes.	
"	13	"	Visit area before XVII Corps Pte	
"	14	"	Reisne Yes.	
"	15	"	31st B.A. A.D.O.S. XVIII C., R.O.M. Yes	
"	16	"	Visited Wilburne Yes	
BLARINGHEM	17	"	55th div Cattle 137th Bn Yes	
"	18	"	Inst Planning Yes.	
"	19	"	60th et Reim Yes	
"	20	"	Visited Omer of Tosmet Chilleup Yes	
"	21	"	& D.D.C.S. Yes	
"	22	"	to be attended Conf of Dep O.C.V. Yes	

WAR DIARY or INTELLIGENCE SUMMARY

Army Form C. 2118.

Place	Date	Hour	Summary of Events and Information	Remarks and references to Appendices
BLARINGHEM	23.2.18		Moved to general HQs	
FREVENT	24		— ERCHEU HQs	
ERCHEU	25		Went to reconnoitre a Bgde. Routine HQs.	
	26		Went to Cavino on L.R. HQs.	
	27		Visits to 59, 60 & 61 Bdes, L.O.C.s HQs	
	28		92nd Bde, N°1 Coy train, Arty T.M. Bde HQs	

Lt. Col. 90 & B.J. 19 B.D.S. 28.2.18

WAR DIARY
INTELLIGENCE SUMMARY

Wadds 20R
Vol 29

Place	Date	Hour	Summary of Events and Information	Remarks and references to Appendices
ERCHEU	1-3-18		Visited A.D.O.S. XVIII Corps. & Lieut. J.A. Msg.	
"	2		A.D.O.S. XVIII Corps. Batto. & Beaucourt Beaulieu and 59th Bn. M.G. Bn.	
"	3		Reg. day.	
"	4		Lecture & Beaucourt & 16/92nd Regt. Inf.	
"	5		Visited HQ Infantry Camp 1/92nd Regt Inf.	
"	6		" 61st Bn., 59th Bn. & 11 R.B. Inf.	
"	7		Visits 11th D.L.I. & 12th Kings Inf.	
"	8		Visits 11th D.L.I. & 12th Kings Inf.	
"	9		Visited A.S.C. Inf.	
"	10		HQ & Amn of Sgt. Mafeen Inf.	
"	11		Inspects Amn of 11th R.B. Regt Inf.	
"	12		" " 11th K.R.R. Inf.	
"	13		" " 2nd Scot. Rifle Inf.	
"	14		Visits Amn on L.P. Inf.	
"	15		Inspects Amn of D.C.L.I. Inf.	
"	16		Visited 91st Regt Inf.	
"	17		" Inspects Amn of 60th T.M.B. Inf.	
"	18		" " " 60th Bde. L.S. Inf.	
"	19		H.Q.S. Beaucourt Latte 60th Bde. W.K.L. Inf.	
"	20		Inspects Sqn L.S. Amn Inf.	
"	21		Lt Col. Bau & St Leny Coy Tak Inf.	

Army Form C. 2118.

WAR DIARY
or
INTELLIGENCE SUMMARY.
(Erase heading not required.)

Instructions regarding War Diaries and Intelligence Summaries are contained in F. S. Regs., Part II. and the Staff Manual respectively. Title pages will be prepared in manuscript.

Place	Date	Hour	Summary of Events and Information	Remarks and references to Appendices
ERCHEU	22-3-18		Visited 5th Army Gun Park. Moved to Beaulieu	
BEAULIEU	23-3-18		Visited XIX Corps. A.D.O.S	
" ROYE	24-3-18		Visited 5th Army Gun Park - Moved to ROYE	
ROYE	25-3-18		Drew V.G's L.G.G. magazines etc. Visited 3rd Gun Park - Drew belts etc	
Moreuil	26-3-18		Visited 5th Army Gun Park. Moved to Quesnel & to Moreuil.	
Domart	27-3-18		Drew L.G's boxes of magazines. Domart	
St Sauflieu	28-3-18		Moved to St Sauflieu	
Remille	29-3-18		" - Remille vers Loeuilly.	
St Loeuy	30-3-18		" - back to St Sauflieu.	
St Sauflieu	31-3-18		Visited XIX Corps -	

Army Form C. 2118

WAR DIARY
or
INTELLIGENCE SUMMARY
(Erase heading not required.)

JA 30

Confidential

War Diary

of

D.A.D.O.S. 20th Dn.

from 1st April, 1918 to 30th April, 1918.

WAR DIARY or INTELLIGENCE SUMMARY

Army Form C. 2118.

Place	Date	Hour	Summary of Events and Information	Remarks and references to Appendices
St Sauflieu	1.4.18		Moves to Briquemesnil. Visited No. 1 Area Laundry, Abbeville. Visited Gun Park (1st Army)	
Briquesnil	2.4.18		Visited Brigades —	
	3.4.18		" 91st Bde R.F.A. & 8th Bde M.G.Bn.	
Liomer	4		Lines to Liomer	
Limeux	5		Visited Roads at Allerey and Forest. 20th M.T. Coy. 59th Bde. Lines to Fouilloy	
"	6		" 91st Bde R.F.A. commenced to refit Bn.	
"	7		Inspected lines of 7 S.L.I., 1st DCLI. and 96 Field Coy.	
"	8		" 61st Bde R.A., 12th Kings, 11th KRRC and 2nd Scot Rif.	
"	9		" 59th " 11th RB, 12th KRRC. Visited O.D.O.S. Huts fire	
Gamaches	10		Visited A.D.O.S. XIX Corps. moved to Huppy thence to Gamaches.	
"	11		Moved into camp. Visited Div Arty HQ.	
"	12		Routine	
"	13		Visited No.1 Laundry, 61st ½ices Ambulance & Div Arty HQ.	
"	14		Inspected lines of 61st Bde HQ, 6th KSLI, and 12 RB.	
"	15		Visited SDG ½ units, Div Arty HQ, & all letters of 92nd Bde.	
"	16		Routine	
"	17		Church Camp	
Mingoval	18		Moves to Mingoval. Visited D.D.O.S. South, at Abbeville en route.	
"	19		Visited Tinques Railhead – Inspected M.G. Bn Transport	
"	20		" Also Baths at Tinques, Cavecourt & Frevillers.	

WAR DIARY or INTELLIGENCE SUMMARY

Army Form C. 2118

Place	Date	Hour	Summary of Events and Information	Remarks and references to Appendices
MINGOVAL	21-4-18		Visited all Inf.y Bdes.	
"	22		Inspected ammn of 12th King's & 7th D.C.L.I.	
"	23		" " 7th Som. L.I. Attended conference at 61st Bde.	
"	24		Went to St. OMER re Laundry	
"	25		Attended conference at 59th Bde. rel. 6th Bde. Inspected ammn of Mot. Vet. Sec.	
"	26		Visited battns at TINQUES & inspected ammn transport of 62nd Field Amb. 61st Field Amb. 12th King's - battns at CAUCOURT & TINQUES.	
"	27			
"	28		5 Rifles brought to Armourer's Shop by 3 different battns, had in every case blown off ends of knobs off, without any sign of damage whatever in the barrel. After careful examination I was unable to arrive at any reasonable explanation so reported the matter to XVIII Corps. The rifles were inspected by the A.D.O.S. who took them to the Corps for further examination.	
"	29		Attended conference of Staff Officers at Q branch, where it was decided to reduce the number of retaining stores, see list attached.	
"	30		During the month of April Army has been supplied without any addition to transport, it has been decided to meet rapidly waves of two Guns by without any team of 250 with and 750 rounds in 6 wagons either of Bde. W.I.T., and similar quantity of own M.T. lorry, this will mean that the reserve will be 500 with and 1500 rounds which in divisions difficult the balance of 200 with and 600 rounds will be retained at Base, the number left here in each Brigade will be used to carry Stokes mortar stores bombs, this will free the limber accommodation so available for ammunition at our Guns magazine to be carried.	

Army Form C. 2118

WAR DIARY or INTELLIGENCE SUMMARY
(Erase heading not required.)

Place	Date	Hour	Summary of Events and Information	Remarks and references to Appendices
MINGOYAL	30-4-18		Ents. Paint recently supplied by Bedes as device colour, is very inferior in shades; there are several greens, some bines, some light slate etc. Many of these shades would do, but an effort should be made to secure uniform in each Division. A.D.S.S. Lieut Col, BEFAOS 20.5.18	
List of Stores referred to under date 29/4/18			The following stores have been withdrawn from Inf.y Batns of this formation:— Breakers, wire, No.1. Boxes, candle, F.S. Cases, No. 1 (or No.2) hot=draughtein Covers " " Frogs, stand, No.1 v 2 Sft Rangefinders, No.1 or 2 Stands, rangefinders, No.1 or 2 Switchboards, Telephone excluding Field Line. Masks, for Lewis Gunners. Boxes, tin, magazine. Pendulum sights for firing rifle Grenades Periscopes. Blocks, tackle, G.S. 1½" Cordage, Double Snatch " " " Discs, signalling, MK II Implements, hatchers:— Balances, spring, 4 lbs Cases, wood, empty Hooks, Dressing, 9 in Lamps, signalling, Electric, Field Hooks, Grenade Stones, tub, scythe Files, longarth, flat, 6 in Jacks, lifting Augers, screw (solid) wring, 1-inch. Pincers, oval, Nos. 21 v 24. Files, regular, cut, hand, 12" Awls, blades, brad. Tools, Edge, No. 2	
Cont'd				

Army Form C. 2118

WAR DIARY
or
INTELLIGENCE SUMMARY
(Erase heading not required.)

Instructions regarding War Diaries and Intelligence Summaries are contained in F.S. Regs., Part II. and the Staff Manual respectively. Title Pages will be prepared in manuscript.

Place	Date	Hour	Summary of Events and Information	Remarks and references to Appendices
Cont'd	List of Stores referred to in xxxx/para 8.		The scale of issue of the following stores has been reduced.	
			Sticks, cleaning, chamber — to 200	
			Axes, felling, curved helve — 12	
			" , hammer headed — 2	
			Hooks, reaping, large — 10	
			Lanterns, tent, folding — 6	
			Crowbars 3'6" — 4	
			Saws, folding, complete — 16	
			Handcuffs, common — 2	
			Reflectors, mirror, S.A. .303 — 12	
			Whistles, Infantry — 48	
			Binoculars, W.P. — 2 per Coy. + 10 per H.Q.	
			Compasses, magnetic — 2 per Coy.	

Cont'd —

Army Form C. 2118

WAR DIARY or INTELLIGENCE SUMMARY

Place	Date	Hour	Summary of Events and Information	Remarks and references to Appendices
Cont. List of Stores w/d. to infty. of 194-18.			The following stores have been withdrawn from the Pioneer batt. of this formation. Chests, tool, filled, bricklayers. Boxes, Carrier, magazine, Lewis Gun. " " " Plumbers. The whole section No. 8 - A " " empty - do - 25 Spares, masons. - do - 26 Points, steel. - do - 29 D Spades, Mk III Chests, tool, filled, Carpenters to be reduced to 10 per Coy. " " " Smiths " 1 per Batt. Saws, folding, complete " 1 " " " " " " 16 " " The scale of issue of the following stores to the M.G. Bn of this formation have been reduced :- Saws, folding, complete to 16 Carriers, ammunition, belt box " 16 The foll. g. stores have been withdrawn :- Compasses, magnetic, pocket. Cans, lubricating, No. 9. Cases, can. 303, Tripod Mountings	[signature] Col $\mathcal{L}$ & Q's BGGS 30-4-18

1875 Wt: W593/826 1,000,000 4/15 J.B.C. & A. A.D.S.S./Forms/C. 2118.

Confidential.
War Diary
of
D.A.D.O.S. 20th Division

from 1st May 1918   to 31st May 1918.

Army Form C. 2118

WAR DIARY
or
INTELLIGENCE SUMMARY

(*Erase heading not required.*)

Instructions regarding War Diaries and Intelligence Summaries are contained in F. S. Regs., Part II. and the Staff Manual respectively. Title Pages will be prepared in manuscript.

Place	Date	Hour	Summary of Events and Information	Remarks and references to Appendices

1875 Wt. W593/826 1,000,000 4/15 J.B.C. & A. A.D.S.S./Forms/C. 2118.

Army Form C. 2118

WAR DIARY or INTELLIGENCE SUMMARY

Place	Date	Hour	Summary of Events and Information	Remarks and references to Appendices
MINGOVAL	1-5-18		Visits Lecount Batt, 1/C.S.L.S., Late New Brackenbury Rifle moved to Villers au Bois Hts.	
VILLERS au BOIS	2 " "		Spent day with Artillery unit J.A.M. Rifle visited battery, enemy's new aircraft MG mounted for Artillery use rifle.	
" "	3 " "		The details for mounting was made how the frame of an indecurable bicycle as follows – See sketch attached.	
" "	4 " "		The bottom bracket of bicycle frame is stripped of everything except the bottom tube, main spindle bearing and rear forks. The ends of the forks are cut off 13" from the bracket and a piece of rod is flat now welded into the ends of each fork. These pieces of rod are bored out, as is Britain to take the trunnions of the gun. The trunnions for B. nature 15, and at D, 5½" long just form a shuttle to keep through left, it is made fast on one side through the other, the end of the first hose pipe is screwed shifts with a wing nut to make the fork be tightened on the gun. The bottom tube A is plugged with a round stud of wood, and a hub spindle # F is inserted into this stud. One bottom of the hub spindle there is a screw cap G in addition to tightening there is the usual fast with a hole bored down from the top to take the title A. This hole is bored to a depth of 12½" or just	

Place	Date	Hour	Summary of Events and Information	Remarks and references to Appendices
VILLERS AU BOIS	4-5.18		Sufficiently deep to prevent the collar E on tube A from resting on the top of the pole. On our view of the pole is left is cut to allow of a transverse driving of castellub, with tall cage being inserted thro' the tall cage is also so that the screws can & work on tall bearings. The setting ? in pole is they push in, but top of pole at I there is a small press plate working on a pivot, the catches the pole to be lowered when the movement is not in place, to prevent rain reaching the tall bearings. When the mounting gun are in position, the running motion bears on low g & as the who-on tell leaving, the gun claw be moved around with great ease. So overcome this difficulty experiences in all existing pole mountings. All the material used can be obtained from almost any salvage dump & any to but together in any but concrete slab. I think it would probably be an improvement if the tall leaving was put under the collar at E, but this would require a special ring of tall cage. MGS	
" SOUCHEZ "	5.5.18 6. 7.		Visited 181 Bde and battn at Auges. MGS Moves to Sheet 36 B x17 central MGS Anxious December transport, invade camp MGS	

WAR DIARY
or
INTELLIGENCE SUMMARY

(Erase heading not required.)

Army Form C. 2118

Place	Date	Hour	Summary of Events and Information	Remarks and references to Appendices
SOUCHEZ	9.5.18		Visited Army Park W/S.	
"	10	"	XIII Corps. O/O 2 Lt. O/S A.D.O.T. inspects card W/S.	
"	11	"	51st Field Amb. 12 St. U.R. St. Paix W/S.	
"	12	"	Fitted breech protector to Lewis rifle. Inspects Rifles serving of this W/S	
"	13	"	Issues to move Lewis from Bn Hds. A.O.C.T. O/S S.A.A. Dis. W/S. Inspects fitted Muzzle protector to rifles of 2nd & 3rd W/S.	
"	14	"	" " " D.C.L.I. W/S.	
"	15	"	overhauls 12 Lewis guns of 2 L.I. W/S	
"	"	"	" " " " " " " " Inspects fitted protectors to rifles of 61st Bde W/S 161st T.M. Bs W/S.	
"	16	"	Overhauled 16 Lewis guns of D.C.L.I. W/S.	
"	17	"	" 12 " " " A.D.O.T. inspects card W/S.	
"	18	"	Visited 60th Bde W/S.	
"	19	"	" 91st Bde. W/S	
"	20	"	" 57th Bde. W/S.	
"	21	"	Overhauls 22 Lewis guns of 12 K.R.R.C. W/S.	
"	22	"	Visits W/S. Examines Lewis Artillery. Inspects rifles & fitted breech protectors 1st K.R.R. W/S.	

Army Form C. 2118

WAR DIARY
or
INTELLIGENCE SUMMARY

(Erase heading not required.)

Instructions regarding War Diaries and Intelligence Summaries are contained in F. S. Regs., Part II. and the Staff Manual respectively. Title Pages will be prepared in manuscript.

Place	Date	Hour	Summary of Events and Information	Remarks and references to Appendices
SOUCHEZ	23.5.18		Inspected lines of 6 K.R.R. & Shelter newangle potation 26 rifles & bayonets workshops	
"	24		Orchards 28 guns (worked)	
"	25		Inspected Coys of 12th R.B. Shelter Newjoy potation, 23 Rifles & bayonets workshops	
"	26		Inspected 24 guns (un-worked) N.R.A.	
"	27		Inspected Coys of 13th KRRC shelter newjoy potation, 6 Rifles & bayonets	
"	28		Visits C.O.M. C.O. Pare on L.P. N.R.	
"	29		C.O.C.S. W.S.	
"	30		" C.O.M.S. Lt. E. C. G. R.A.L. 12th R.B. 13th KRRC 10 Middle W.S.	
"	31		" M.G. Bn. L.G.V. R.A. M.S.	
			" By 24: Bn leaves M.S.	
			" C.O.C.S. Inspects camps. Busiest tewds for intakes of any mem. W.	

[signature] Major Gent
B.A.D.D.S. 20 93
3-5-18.
B.A.

Confidential.

War Diary
of
D.A.D.O.S. 20th Division.

from 1st June 1918.   to 30th June 1918.

Army Form C. 2118.

WAR DIARY
or
INTELLIGENCE SUMMARY.

(Erase heading not required.)

Instructions regarding War Diaries and Intelligence Summaries are contained in F. S. Regs., Part II. and the Staff Manual respectively. Title pages will be prepared in manuscript.

Place	Date	Hour	Summary of Events and Information	Remarks and references to Appendices

A5834   Wt. W4973 M687 750,000 8/16   D. D. & L. Ltd.   Forms/C.2118/13.

Army Form C. 2118

WAR DIARY
or
INTELLIGENCE SUMMARY
(Erase heading not required.)

Place	Date	Hour	Summary of Events and Information	Remarks and references to Appendices
Sow #52	1-6-18		The want of authentic quantity of parts. Drew attention of DOS to this matter. Inspected arms of 2nd Scottish Rifles rifles muzzle protectors, 56 Rifles to reclaim, 22 bayonets to exchange. Inspected rifles of 11th KRR rifles muzzle protectors, 66 rifles for reclaim. Inspected rifles of 59th Bn LB 18 rifles for exchange, Inspected rifles of 11th RB rifles muzzle protectors, 48 rifles and 9 bayonets to exchange. Overhauls 28 Lewis guns of 11th KRR & 20 of 2nd S.R. ffsg. Overhauls 24 Lewis guns of 11th R.B. ffsg. Visited Gun Park ffsg. Overhauls 16 Vickers guns of 20th M.G. Bn. D.O.O.S. inspects camp ffsg.	
"	2	"	" " " " " " ffsg.	
"	3	"	Inspected rifles of	
"	4	"	Inspected rifles 123 Lewis guns of 12th Kings. 33 rifles 112 bayonets exchange ffsg.	
"	5	"	" 28 " " 7 D.C.L.I. 46 rifles 9 bayonets " ffsg.	
"	6	"	" 32 " " 7 Som L.I. 59 " +5 " " ffsg.	
"	7	"	Held new attachments for 36 Grenade Discharges ffsg.	
"	8	"		
"	9	"		
"	10	"		
"	11	"		

WAR DIARY or INTELLIGENCE SUMMARY

Army Form C. 2118

Place	Date	Hour	Summary of Events and Information	Remarks and references to Appendices
SOUTHEZ	12.6.19		Coleplis Ramsay lines for new clasp photos taken by reverse. Graduates photo taken, new graduations to agree with MK v Jubilees on reverse side. /ffg.	
	13.6.19		Altered photo notice boards by fitting wale slide to prevent collar slipping. Swell recesses in gun to prevent collar shifting. /ffg. Visited B92. /ffg.	
	14 "		"	
	15 "		Fuel lining workshop. /ffg.	
	16 "		Green Park. 1e.O.O.S. /ffg.	
	17 "		Tests new attachment for discharge cup. Test very unsatisfactory /ffg.	
	18 "		Visits A.O.O.S. O.O.C.T. LOD 24.e Div /ffg.	
	19 "		Inspects Lewis Guns of K.S.L.I. 42 Rifles obtained 36 exchanged 5 keypoints collars /ffg.	
	20 "		Visits IV Corps Gas school /ffg.	
	21 "		Inspects arms + 30 Lewis guns of 12 R.B. 46 rifles obtained, 16 exchanged 5 keypoint collars /ffg. " " 2 Revolver obtained 1 Society /ffg.	
	22 "		" 32 " - 12 KRR 22 " - 13 " 6 "
			" " - 60 Bledd 3 " - 4 " /ffg.
			" " - 60 T.M.B 12 " - 3 " /ffg.
			A.B.Cup 12 K.R.R.C. 30 " - 13 " /ffg.
	23 "		Visits N°2 Area laundry at Orcq /ffg.	
	24 "			
	25 "		Visits M.T. Coy. Arranges a slightly altered discharge attachment for N°36 grenade. /ffg.	

WAR DIARY
or
INTELLIGENCE SUMMARY

Army Form C. 2118

Place	Date	Hour	Summary of Events and Information	Remarks and references to Appendices
SOUCHEZ	26.6.18		Inspected Linesmen jobs delivering chaulk ffs.	
"	27		Visited 60 & 161st Bde HQs ffs.	
"	28		Inspected lewis gun of 11th KRR. 65 rifle refinished indefair. 25 rifles 113 bayonets recleaned ffs. 2 revolvers clainoffs.	
"	29		" " 31 " " 2nd S.R. 78 " " 25 " " " ffs.	
"	30		" " 16 " " B.O Corps 11 RB. 30 " " 10 " 28 " " ffs.	

Major ... t. O.S.
D.A.O.S. 20

WAR DIARY or INTELLIGENCE SUMMARY

Army Form C. 2118

DADOS 20D
Vol 33

Place	Date	Hour	Summary of Events and Information	Remarks and references to Appendices
Souez H.F.Z	1-7-18		Inspects Arms + 14 Lewis guns of A+C Corps, 11 R.B. 37 rifles repaired at inspection	Apps.
"	2		" " " 59th T.M.B.s 7 " " "	Apps.
"	3		" " " 59 Bde H.Q. 1 " " "	Apps.
"	4		Visits 59th Bde H.Q.	Apps.
"	5		Duties inspected by A.D.O.S.	Apps.
"	6		Visits 59 Bde H.Q.	Apps.
"	7		" 61 "	Apps.
"	7		Inspects Arms of 12th Kings, 36 Rifles + 2 revolvers repaired at inspection, 10 rifles + 18 bayonets exchanged	Apps.
"	8		Overhauled 31 Lewis guns of 7 Som L.I. 2 weeks duty neglected	Apps.
"	8		" 31 " " 7 D.C.L.I. Condition good.	Apps.
"	9		Inspects Arms of 7 Som L.I. 48 rifles repaired at inspection, 19 rifles + 2 bayonets exchanged	Apps.
"	9		" " 7 D.C.L.I. 40 " " " 19 " 3 "	Apps.
"	10		Overhauled 25 Lewis guns of 12th Kings. 1 weeks duty neglected	Apps.
"	11		Inspects Arms of 61st Bde H.Q. Condition good	Apps.
"	12		Visits 61st Bde H.Q. Shenshot line	Apps.
"	13		Visits Gun Park	Apps.
"	14		Inspects Arms of 61st T.M.B.s 10 repairs at inspection	Apps.
"	15		Inspects all rifles of 61st Bde	Apps.
"	15		Visits No. 2 Area Laundry St Blue	Apps.
"	16		60th Bde 16. 1st Field Amb. Inspects arms of 6 KSLI. 35 Rifles repaired at inspection. 8 rifles + 7 bayonets exchanged	Apps.
"	16		Inspects Q.M. stores of all Infty Bns. Inspects arms of 12 KRR. 24 rifles + 13 bayonets repaired	Apps.
"	17		exchanged condition reps. " 2 Lewis guns of 6 KSLI inspected. Condition good	Apps.

WAR DIARY or INTELLIGENCE SUMMARY

Army Form C. 2118

Place	Date	Hour	Summary of Events and Information	Remarks and references to Appendices
SOUCHEZ	18.7.18		Inspected arms of 12" R.B. 50 rifles repaired at inspection - 6 rifles exchanged	
"	19		"Lewis" overhauled 35 " Cartridge Sorter.	
			Cartridges Sorted with the reception of 1 Gun. Inspected arms of 61" T.M.B. 8 rifles repairs on inspection. 1 rifle + 1 bayonet exchanged. Cartridge Sort.	
			Inspected arms of 60" Bde H.Q. Cartridge Sort. 5 rifles repairs on inspection. 1 rifle + 1 bayonet exchanges.	
"	20		Visited Div Q+G also R.A + 60" Bde. H.Q.	
"	21		Inspected bicycles of H.Q. S.S.S. Anything reqd. to complete batteries with 4 Lewis Guns per battery. Part repaired 16. Visited A.D.O.S VIII Corps. 16 Lewis Guns & 88 magazine boxes received from Army Dept.	
"	22			
"	23		Routine. Has stores in yard of the camp rolled by steam roller. Visited 61" Bde. H.Q.	
"	24		Routine.	
"	25		Visited Div 'Q' 'G' + R.A., also A.D.O.S VIII Corps. Inspected arms of 11" K.R.R.C. 14 rifles + 6 bayonets exchanged. 32 rifles repaired at inspection. 3 reviews repaired. Cartridge Sort.	
"	26		A.D.O.S VIII Corps visited Dump. Visited 59" Bde. Inspected arms of 2 Scot Rif Cartridge Sort. 29 rifles + 23 bayonets to repair. 6.5 Rifles repaired on inspection. 36 Lewis Guns of 11 KRRC overhauled in shop. Cartridge Sort.	
"	27		Inspected arms of 11" R.B. Cartridge Sort. 11 rifles + 7 bayonets exchanged. 20 rifles repaired at inspection. 32 Lewis Guns overhauled.	
"	28		VIII Corps Commander inspected Camp expressed Satisfaction. Inspected arms of 59" T.M.B. Cartridge Sort. 2 rifles + 3 bayonets exchanged. 3 rifle repairs at inspection. 59" Bde HQ " " 4 " " 3 bayonets	
"	29		36 Lewis Guns of 11" RB overhauled. Cartridge Sort.	
"	30		Visited 59" Bde, Div Q + Arty HQ.	
"	31		Routine.	

Holborn Hele ? Dis
O. A.D.O.S. 2.8.18

WAR DIARY

INTELLIGENCE SUMMARY

D.A.D.O.S.

Army Form C. 2118

WD 34

Place	Date	Hour	Summary of Events and Information	Remarks and references to Appendices
SOUCHEZ	1.8.15		Routine	
	2 "		Returns now been [illeg.]	
	3 "		Inspected Guns of 7th Div. C.S. 30 rifles & 1 revolver returned at inspection 15 rifles & 1 bayonet exchanged. Appx.	
	4 "		" " 15th King's 40 " + 2 " 15 " 17 " Appx. Inspected 34 Brig. guns of 2ng C.S. condition only fair. Appx. Visited Right & left sectors of 15th Bde. Appx.	
	5 "		Inspected 32 Bn. guns of 15th Brig. condition good. Appx. Inspected guns of 1 D.C.L.I. 6 rifles & 12 Hotchkiss refunds at inspection 15 rifles & bayonets exchanged. Appx. Visited A.D.O.S. Appx.	
	6 "		Inspected 35 Brig. guns of 6th T.M.B. 12 rifles refunds at inspection 3 rifles & bayonets exchanged Appx. Inspected Guns of 61st T.M.B. 2 " " Appx. " 61st Bde M.G. 2 " " Appx.	
	7 "		Inspected bicycles of King's 7. Somersets 9. Cornwalls 9. 6th T.M.Bs 2. 61st Bde M.G. 2. Appx. 61st Bde sig sec 6. Appx.	
	8 "		Visited SEBRU on L.P. Appx.	
	9 "		Visited 97th Bde Appx.	
	10 "		Inspected Guns of 2nd corps D.A.S. 40 refunds at inspection 15 rifles & 11 bayonets exchanged Appx.	
	11 "		Overhauled 11 Lewis guns of D.A.S. condition good Appx.	

WAR DIARY
INTELLIGENCE SUMMARY

(Erase heading not required.)

Army Form C. 2118

Instructions regarding War Diaries and Intelligence Summaries are contained in F.S. Regs., Part II. and the Staff Manual respectively. Title Pages will be prepared in manuscript.

Place	Date	Hour	Summary of Events and Information	Remarks and references to Appendices
SOUCHEZ	12.8.18		Inspected arms of 8th D.L.I. H.Q & Transport. Condition of H.Q rifles very good. Transport .. dirty, 2 rifles & 1 bayonet for exchange. 12 rifles repaired at inspection.	
"	13.8.18		Arms of 1st K.S.L.I. Condition good. Visited 83rd Feed Coy ref: extra transport stores, serving guns, 29 rifles repaired at inspection. 12 rifles & 4 bayonets for exchange. R.8	
"	14.8.18		Inspected arms of 12th K.R.R.C. Condition good. 14 rifles & 18 bayonets for exchange. 25 " repaired at inspection. R.L	
"	15.8.18		Visited A.D.O.S VIII Corps. Inspected arms of 12th R.B. Condition Good. 14 rifles & 5 bayonets for exchange. 45 rifles repaired at inspection.	N.2.
"	16.8.18		34 Lewis guns of 12th R.B overhauled in the shop. Condition Good.	R.B.
"	17.8.18		Inspected arms of 'B' Coy N.D.L.I. Condition good. 4 rifles & 11 bayonets exchanged. 35 rifles repaired at inspection.	N.R.
"	18.8.18		A.D.O.S. visited Dump. Inspected bicycle of 161 Coy A.S.C. Condition good.	N.
"	19.8.18		Visited 69th Bde. Inspected 8 bicycles of 12th R.B. Condition fair.	N.R.
"	20.8.18		A.D.O.S VIII Corps & R.O.O AUBIGNY. Inspected arms of 2nd P.Rifles. Condition Good. 21 Rifles & 2 bayonets for exchange. 35 rifles repaired at inspection.	N.L.
"	21.8.18		36 Lewis Guns of 2nd Foot R.y overhauled. Condition Good with the exception of 3 Guns. R.B. Repaired 1 Lewis Gun of 7th Son. C.I.I.	
"	22.8.18		Inspected arms of 'A' Coy 20th Bn M.G.C. Condition v.good. 5 rifles & 2 bayonets exchanged. 18 " repaired at inspection.	N.L
"	23.8.18		Inspected Q.M. stores of all Infantry battns.	
"	24 "		Inspected arms of 6th K.S.L.I. 2 revolvers & 40 rifles repaired at inspection. 12 rifles & 1 bayonet exchanged. 144. Overhauled 53 Lewis Guns of 6th K.S.L.I. Condition 4 to 6 others Good. Lc99.	
"	25 "		Visited 61st Bde. dungeons hall 1/99.	

Army Form C. 2118

Instructions regarding War Diaries and Intelligence Summaries are contained in F.S. Regs., Part II. and the Staff Manual respectively. Title Pages will be prepared in manuscript.

WAR DIARY
INTELLIGENCE SUMMARY
(Erase heading not required.)

Place	Date	Hour	Summary of Events and Information	Remarks and references to Appendices
SOUCHEZ	26.8.18		Inspected 6th K.S.L.I. Mds. Inspected bicycle of 2nd Scots Rif., 7 S.L.I. & 6 K.S.L.I. Mds.	
"	27	"	Inspected Cans of B Coy. M.G. Bn. 12 rifles repaired at inspection, 3 rifles recharged, found in good condition. Mds.	
"	28	"	Visited C.O.O.S. and 59th Bde. Mds.	
"	29	"	Inspected Cans of 12th Kings, 64 rifles repaired at inspection, 15 rifles returned. rechamped Mds. ordered return Cans of 12th Kings condition good Mds.	
"	30	"	" 15 " " " Issued SO 789/42 to units. this at stamp 23.9.15. asked to ease emergency Mds. Inspected Cans of 114 R.B. 30 rifles repaired at inspection, 17 rifles 9 repairs rechamp. Mds.	
"	31	"	Visited Ordnance 24 Div. Inspected Kings transport, Inspected 4 platoon of the Artillery who has had 2 days training in Div. Armourer shop on live fires, seems to conclusion 2 days was not enough. Mds.	

Signature D.A.D.O.S. 24 Div.
31.8.15

Confidential.

War Diary

D.A.D.O.S. 20th Division

from 1st September, 1918.   to 30th September, 1918.

Army Form C. 2118.

WAR DIARY
or
INTELLIGENCE SUMMARY.
(Erase heading not required.)

Instructions regarding War Diaries and Intelligence Summaries are contained in F. S. Regs., Part II. and the Staff Manual respectively. Title pages will be prepared in manuscript.

Place	Date	Hour	Summary of Events and Information	Remarks and references to Appendices

DADOS 20D

Army Form C. 2118.

VR 35

WAR DIARY
or
INTELLIGENCE SUMMARY.
(Erase heading not required.)

Place	Date	Hour	Summary of Events and Information	Remarks and references to Appendices
SOUCHEZ	1-9-18		Event of enquiry re horse [illegible] lost by Knips [illegible]	
"	2	"	Inspects W.T.S. of O.C. 1 [illegible]	
"	3	"	Inspects arms of 11/R.B., conducted 30 twin guns [illegible], receipt 86680 whole	
			in duty return from report. Visited 60/61 Bon [illegible]	
"	4	"	Inspects armorer's shop of 11/42 KRR, 11/42 R.B., 2 S.R. 6 KSLI. 12 Kings 7 North [illegible]	
			7 D.C.L.I. & 20 M.G.B. Visited J.O.M. 33 MT [illegible]	
"	5	"	Inspects armorer's shops of 11 O.E.J. 60, 61, 62 Bus Bn. A.B.C.D/92 A.C/91. also	
			Q.M. store of above units [illegible]	
"	6	"	Inspects transport of D.C.I. M.G. Coy. Kings 12 KRR. 11 R.B. 18 & 30 Bus. Coy. [illegible]	
			Inspects rifles of 7 D.C.L.I. 70 rifles returned at Felshetin, 12 rifles at transport[illegible] Returns [illegible]	
			Ordered 18 twin guns of 7 D.C.I. and return 600 [illegible]	
"	7	"	" 18 " " " Inspects 8 heaps of DCI. and twin gun [illegible]	
			Inspects arms of 11/4 KRR. 72 rifle reported infants 13 rifle 2 bayonets to armorer workshop [illegible]	
"	8	"	Ordered 30 twin guns of 11 KRR. and twin gun receipt 72466 which on duty [illegible]	
"	9	"	" 36 " " " - 28894 + 56883 duty respects return [illegible]	
			" 12 R.B.	
"	10	"	Inspects arms of 12 R.B. 42 rifle returned at infants brifle 13 bayonet returns [illegible]	
			Ordered 7 bicycles of 11 KRR. C.C. of 12 R.B. and twin guns [illegible]	
"	11	"	Visited No 2 base laundry. Arms & mounting of Cellule to Busin. A.A. [illegible]	
"	12	"	Visited A.O.D., M.T.Coy, J.O.M. [illegible]	
"	13	"	Instructs class for instruction of Sewing in Lewis guns. 3 days course is not	
			[illegible] a very materially increased [illegible]	

Army Form C. 2118.

WAR DIARY
or
INTELLIGENCE SUMMARY.
(Erase heading not required.)

Place	Date	Hour	Summary of Events and Information	Remarks and references to Appendices
SOUCHEZ	14-9-18		Inspected Coy of 7 Sorn L.I. 61 rifle ulaido &fistolas 11 Rifle do bayonets & 1 numtin rectangs Mo. Ordered 18 twin pms of 7 Som. L.I. godstin prod Mo.	
"	15		"	
"	16		Inspected Coys of 6th K.S.L.I. 52 rifle ulaido&chistolain 11 rifle & bayonet rectangs Mo. 6 bayts of 7 Som L.I. Condition Smd Mo. Ordered 35 twin pms of 6th K.S.L.I. Condem prod Mo. 7 bayts	
"	17		Inspected Coys of 2nd S.R. 82 Rifle ulain + 7 rifle + 15 bayonet rectangs. Condition fair not sufficient attention is paid to cleaning of bones Mo. Ordered 36 twin pms of 2nd S.R. Condition smd, but saw still be damage thut.	
"	"		Every Chum roon lance Mo. Inspected 9 bayts of 2nd S.R. Condition smd. Mo.	
"	18		Visited G.O.C. 60th Bde Mo.	
"	19		Wounded Conference at C.O.O. Mo.	
"	20			
"	21		GOOD conference Mo.	
"	22		Inspected transport of O.T.S. A.G.B. Mo. Inspected Coys of Kings 38 rifle ulains 2 rifle & 5 bayonets rectangs Mo.	
"	23		Ordered 33 twin pns of Kings Condition smd except N° 90429 very dity Mo. Inspected Coys of 12 KRR 63 rifle ulains 9 rifle & 11 bayonet rectangs Mo. 35 twin pns of 12th KRR Condition and excelt N° 38893 very dity, neglets Mo.	

Army Form C. 2118.

WAR DIARY
or
INTELLIGENCE SUMMARY.
(Erase heading not required.)

Instructions regarding War Diaries and Intelligence Summaries are contained in F. S. Regs., Part II. and the Staff Manual respectively. Title pages will be prepared in manuscript.

Place	Date	Hour	Summary of Events and Information	Remarks and references to Appendices
SOWGHEZ	24.9.19		Inspects Q.M. Store of M.G. Bn. & D.L.I. visits I.O.M. lines.	
"	25	"	Inspects Guard of 11th R.B. 49 rifles & workshops, 9 rifles & bayonets & camp lines. Inspects Guard of Kings L.I. 23 K.R.R. Kitchen 1000 lbs.	
"	26	"	Orders to Lewis Guns of 11th R.B. Kitchen. Inspects receipt 81992 duty ninety lbs. Inspects Rifles of 11th R.B. Kitchen 1000 lbs.	
"	27	"	Visits O & 58 Ors. Inspects Q.M. Store of Mot. C.L. See lbs.	
"	28	"	Inspects vehicles of Mob. C.L. Ac. visits M.T. Bde.	
"	29	"	Inspects Guard of 7th O.C.C.I. 38 Rifle retains, 9 Rifles, 5 bayonets exchanged, 1 revolver & 1 bayt. Orders to 19 Lewis Guns of O.C.L. Kitchen 1800 lbs. Kitchen retains lbs.	
			7 Bayets of O.C.L.S. Kitchen lbs.	
"	30	"	9 Lewis Guns of O.C.L.S. Kitchen good receipt No. 92395 & 70904 which were ditto ninety three of touring lbs.	
			Our advance in this area has demonstrated the advantages of having the Ordnance dump close to unit dumps. Stonelot lines. We were able to work a system of letter visitations as follows:– A battalion on relief gives into it next camp about 2 A.M. It's men are usually allowed to rest till about 9 A.M. they then draw of Lewis equipment etc at 2 how our Company send 2 festoon & my count on to its lethe, to	

Army Form C. 2118.

WAR DIARY
or
INTELLIGENCE SUMMARY.
(Erase heading not required.)

Place	Date	Hour	Summary of Events and Information	Remarks and references to Appendices
			This is very rough but they have inflicted minor injuries considerable rifles on enthroughts the det. At 2.30 the two lots of section clamp on, in the platoon at both ran her the platoon had fd to both. At 3 pm. another lay is trails in the hen way, at to cavalry ret 5 months. Buth at 6 am. all the Bu has the cas to the humorism sloh at 8.30 AM. all the units during the day. This means that the Bu is letter-inelects we own day is free to so as with transmy for the helene of the next trenches. Being close to unit lands all so have been long transport because until new solvent than so seefy it enables we to watch. OMs than men carefully. Have here pat much more smoothly under this condition than when my help was then to bis life. Memory has write.	

M Brown. Major
O.A.O.O.S. 20th Div.
30.9.18.

WAR DIARY
or
INTELLIGENCE SUMMARY.
(Erase heading not required.)

Army Form C. 2118.

DANTS 2/36
18 36

Place	Date	Hour	Summary of Events and Information	Remarks and references to Appendices
BOUCHEZ	1-10-18		Visits I.O.S. I.O.O.S. I.O.M. Gen. Pal. Hqs.	
"	2 "		Instructs transport of all div. to Bouzy Hqs.	
"	3 "		Visits all bttns in new area Hqs.	
"	4 "		Visits 5th & 15th Bde Hqs Hqs.	
"	5 "		Visit to new area Hqs.	
MINGOVAL	6 "		moves to Mingoval Hqs.	
"	7 "		Receives issue of Beaulé Hqs.	
"	8 "		Instructs bns. drain fund of 11th RB. 35 Rifles & bayns 2 rifle & 5 bayonets exchanged	
			Condition of arm good. Receives first set of wire clothing Hqs.	
			Inspects Camp Office. Drain fund of 2nd S.R. 30 rifles & bayns, 23 rifles & bayonets & revolvers	
			exchanged. Drain fund 4P 78119 retained.	
"	9 "		Inspects bns drain fund of 12th Kings 4 rifle exchanged; bn bttn Hqs	
				7th D.C.L.I. 1 revolver retained. 8 rifle & bayonets exchanged
			Condition fair Hqs.	
"	10 "		Inspects bns. drain fund of 4th 13 KRR. 12 Rifles exchanged, 1 Lewis gun retained Hqs.	
			" " " 6th KSLI. 5 rifle & 2 bayonets " 1 " " " " Hqs.	
"	11 "		" " " 12 RB. 30 rifle & bayonet retained 12 rifle & bayonet exchanged Hqs.	

Army Form C. 2118.

WAR DIARY
or
INTELLIGENCE SUMMARY.
(Erase heading not required.)

Instructions regarding War Diaries and Intelligence Summaries are contained in F.S. Regs., Part II. and the Staff Manual respectively. Title pages will be prepared in manuscript.

Place	Date	Hour	Summary of Events and Information	Remarks and references to Appendices
MINGOVAL	12.10.18		Inspects C'mm. turn over of R.E.E. 12 rifles 12 bayonets spearmp. 2 knives fm 2 wooden refairs HQ	
"	"		" 9th Field Coy. 40 rifles refairs, 15 rifles & bayonets rec. amp "	
"	"		" 96 " " 36 " 14 " 2 " "	
"	"		" 7th S.or. S. 15 " 4 " "	
"	13 "		" 11th D.T.S. 40 " 32 " "	
"	"		" 85° Field Coy. 10 " 6 " "	
"	14 "		Went to Div. Catg. H.Q.	
"	15 "		" D.O.S. 1st Army. H.Q.	
"	16 "		Attended G.C.M. at 6th Bn. H.Q. H.Q.	
"	17 "		Routine H.Q.	
"	18 "		Went to Dis. Cay. H.Q.	
"	19 "		Routine H.Q.	
"	20 "		Went to Div. Catg. H.Q.	
"	21 "		Visited 61st Bde. H.Q.	
"	22 "		" 59th " "	
"	23 "		Inspects 11th K.R.R. H.Q.	
"	24 "		Visits 60th Bde. H.Q.	
"	25 "		" Artillery H.Q.	

Army Form C. 2118.

WAR DIARY
or
INTELLIGENCE SUMMARY.
(Erase heading not required.)

Instructions regarding War Diaries and Intelligence Summaries are contained in F. S. Regs., Part II. and the Staff Manual respectively. Title pages will be prepared in manuscript.

Place	Date	Hour	Summary of Events and Information	Remarks and references to Appendices
MINGOVAL	26.10.18		Subjects M.G. Bn. lks.	
"	27	"	Routine lks.	
"	28	"	Subjects L.K.S.+I.J. lks.	
"	29	"	Chains dump for range lks.	
CAMBRAI	30	"	Moves to Cambrai lks.	
"	31	"	Lecture @ batts, stores, clot, etc lks.	

Major Leys i/c Ops.
B.A.O.O 20. Ops.
31.10.18.

Confidential.

War Diary
of
D.A.D.O.S. 20th Div.

from 1st November 1918. 30th November 1918.

Army Form C. 2118.

WAR DIARY
or
INTELLIGENCE SUMMARY.

(Erase heading not required.)

Instructions regarding War Diaries and Intelligence Summaries are contained in F. S. Regs., Part II. and the Staff Manual respectively. Title pages will be prepared in manuscript.

Place	Date	Hour	Summary of Events and Information	Remarks and references to Appendices

D. D. & L., London, E.C.
(A'o01) Wt. W1771/M2031 7500/00 5/17 **Sch. 52** Forms C2.-6/14

Army Form C. 2118.

WAR DIARY
or
INTELLIGENCE SUMMARY.
(Erase heading not required.)

Instructions regarding War Diaries and Intelligence Summaries are contained in F. S. Regs., Part II. and the Staff Manual respectively. Title pages will be prepared in manuscript.

Place	Date	Hour	Summary of Events and Information	Remarks and references to Appendices
CAMBRAI	1.11.18		Went to railhead Marcoing	
"	2		Visited 6½ Bde.	
"	3		" - went to railhead Marcoing	
RIEUX	4		" 6½ - "	
			Moved to RIEUX. Visited 7th DCLI	
AVESNES-le-AUBERT	5		Moved to AVESNES-les-AUBERT. Visited 60 Bde & railhead CAMBRAI, also Art. Gun Park	
VENDEGIES	6		" " VENDEGIES. Visited 60 Bde & all batts.	
WARGNIES-le-Grand	7		" Visited Arty. WARGNIES-le-Grand	
WARGNIES-le-grand	8		Moved to WARGNIES-le-Grand.	
BAVAY	9		" " BAVAY	
"	10		Went to arrange a dump for next move.	
FEIGNIES	11		Moved to FEIGNIES. Solesmes & to rear dump Cambrai.	
"	12		Went to railhead Solesmes & to rear dump Cambrai.	
"	13		Inspected Dickers Group 20 B.M.G.C. A & B Coys. Condition v. satisfactory.	
"	14		Went to railhead Solesmes & to rear dump Cambrai.	
"	15		Routine.	
"	16		"	
"	17		Went to railhead Solesmes & to Rieis Auber.	
"	18		Visited 61st Bde & 61st Rieis Auber.	
"	19		Went to railhead Solesmes & rear dump Cambrai. Visited 57/92 RFA	
"	20		Visited 6 KSLI.	
"	21		Went to railhead Solesmes & rear dump Cambrai, also XVII Corps Arthur Rch.gr.	

Army Form C. 2118.

WAR DIARY
or
INTELLIGENCE SUMMARY.
(Erase heading not required.)

Instructions regarding War Diaries and Intelligence Summaries are contained in F. S. Regs., Part II. and the Staff Manual respectively. Title pages will be prepared in manuscript.

Place	Date	Hour	Summary of Events and Information	Remarks and references to Appendices
FEIGNIES	22.11.18.		Went to Railhead Solesmes. Prepared for move.	
CAMBRAI.	23.11.18.		Moved to CAMBRAI. Went to railhead between St AUBERT.	
"	24.11.18		Went to railhead, St AUBERT - O.O. XVII C.T.	
"	25.11.18.		Went to Div. H.Q at Wargnies-le-Grand.	
"	26.11.18.		" at RIEUX, also to railhead St AUBERT.	
"	27.11.18		Went to ACHEUX to find dump for next move. Despatched stores re by trucks to new area.	
"	28.11.18		A.D.O.S XVII Corps v D.D.O.S 3rd Army.	
ACHEUX.	29.11.18		Moved to ACHEUX.	
"	30.11.18		Routine.	

Confidential.
War Diary
of
D.A.D.O.S. 20th Division

from 1st December 1918.   to 31st December 1918.

Army Form C. 2118.

WAR DIARY
or
INTELLIGENCE SUMMARY.

(Erase heading not required.)

Instructions regarding War Diaries and Intelligence Summaries are contained in F. S. Regs., Part II. and the Staff Manual respectively. Title pages will be prepared in manuscript.

Place	Date	Hour	Summary of Events and Information	Remarks and references to Appendices

(AS001) Wt. W1771/M2031 750,000 5/17 **Sch. 52** Forms C2-0/14

D. D. & L., London, E.C.

WAR DIARY
or
INTELLIGENCE SUMMARY.
(Erase heading not required.)

Army Form C. 2118.

DADVS 20 Vol 38

Place	Date	Hour	Summary of Events and Information	Remarks and references to Appendices
ACHEUX	1-12-18		Moved Quarters to ACHEUX.	
"	2.12.18		Went to railhead, Doullens, & D.H.Q at Pas. Visited M.T. Coy workshops.	
"	3.12.18		Went to M.T.Coy workshops.	
"	4.12.18		Visited 60th + 61st Bdes + 6 K.S.L.I + 12 King's.	
"	5.12.18		Went to railhead, Doullens.	
"	6.12.18		Went to D.H.Q at Pas + railhead Doullens.	
"	7.12.18		Visited 61st Bde.	
"	8.12.18		Routine.	
"	9.12.18		Visited 92nd Bde R.F.A + D.H.Q.	
"	10.12.18		Visited 59th Bde Lavangis Detaining Chamber.	
"	11.12.18		6 K.S.L.I. 60 Bde. D.H.Q	
"	12.12.18		59 Bde, 11 K.R.R.C. Detaining Chamber. 6 K.S.L.I. 12 K.R.R.C 7 D.C.L.I, Lattoy + 12. R.B.	
"	13.12.18		61st Bde + Baths near Vaudelles.	
"	14.12.18		Detaining Chamber at 12 K.R.R.C. at Courin.	
"	15.12.18		D.H.Q, Arty. H.Q, Batts Gaudreinpré, 92nd Bde R.F.A Crosyz	
"	16.12.18		M.G. Bn, 7 Somerset L.I + 7 D.C.L.I	
"	17.12.18		D.H.Q, 6th K.S.L.I, 61st Bde.	

Army Form C. 2118.

WAR DIARY
or
INTELLIGENCE SUMMARY.
(Erase heading not required.)

Instructions regarding War Diaries and Intelligence Summaries are contained in F. S. Regs., Part II. and the Staff Manual respectively. Title pages will be prepared in manuscript.

Place	Date	Hour	Summary of Events and Information	Remarks and references to Appendices
ACHEUX	18-12-18		Went to R.A.H.Q. & 92nd Bde R.F.A.	
"	19.12.18		Went to 12th Kings, 12th KRRC, 6th Bde H.Q.	
"	20.12.18		Went to 63rd Bde, 6 KSLI, D.H.Q.	
"	21.12.18		Went to 12 KRRC, 6KSLI 6th Bde	
"	22.12.18		Routine	
"	23.12.18		Went to D.H.Q. & 92nd Bde R.F.A.	
"	24.12.18		Went to Amiens on L.P.	
"	25.12.18		Routine	
"	26.12.18		Went to O.O 17 C.Tp.	
"	27.12.18		Routine	
"	28.12.18		Went to Conference at Ord. XVII Corps	
"	29.12.18		Routine	
"	30.12.18		Visited 59 Bde. 11 R.B. 11 KRRC & 2 For.Rif.	
"	31.12.18		Routine	

31/1/18 [signatures] D.T.P.J.S. 20 BN

Army Form C. 2118.

WAR DIARY
or
INTELLIGENCE SUMMARY.
(Erase heading not required.)

DADOS 20

Place	Date	Hour	Summary of Events and Information	Remarks and references to Appendices
ACHEUX	1.1.19		Visited Hd. 96th Field Coy R.E. ~ Sy Boe.	
"	2.1.19		Went to Amiens. L.P.	
"	3.1.19		Visited G.H.S.L.I	
"	4.1.19		Went to D.H.Q. 12th Kings.	
"	5.1.19		Routine	
"	6.1.19		Visited 60th Bde H.Q. & G.H.S.L.I Q.M. Stores	
"	7.1.19		Routine	
"	8.1.19		Visited 160 Coy A.S.C. & 12th R.B.	
"	9.1.19		R.A.H.Q. D.T.M.O, 92nd Bde H.Q., B/92, 158 Coy Train, 1 Sec D.A.C, 32nd D.V.A.Col, &c.	
"	10.1.19		Routine	
"	11.1.19		Visited 7th Corps.	
"	12.1.19		Routine	
"	13.1.19		Visited 12th R.B.	
"	14.1.19		Visited 61st Inf Bde.	
"	15.1.19		Routine	
"	16.1.19		Visited A.D.O.S. 17 Corps & 12th R.B.	
"	17.1.19		Visited 61st Inf Bde & 12th R.B.	
"	18.1.19		Visited ADOS 17 Corps, Q. Divn, 20th Bn M.G.C.	
"	19.1.19		Routine	
"	20.1.19		Visited 59th Bde H.Q. 11th R.B. 11th KRRC & 12th KRRC	

Army Form C. 2118.

WAR DIARY
or
INTELLIGENCE SUMMARY.
(Erase heading not required.)

Instructions regarding War Diaries and Intelligence Summaries are contained in F. S. Regs., Part II. and the Staff Manual respectively. Title pages will be prepared in manuscript.

Place	Date	Hour	Summary of Events and Information	Remarks and references to Appendices
ACHEUX	21.1.19		Visited Div. H.Q.	
"	22.1.19		"	
"	23.1.19		Visited Div. H.Q. Went to Amiens. L.P.	
"	24.1.19		Visited 11. R.B.	
"	25.1.19		Went to Ordnance, Calais.	
"	26.1.19		Returned from " — Went round H.Q.	
"	27.1.19		Went to H.Q 17 Corps & to Conference at 3rd Army.	
"	28.1.19		Visited A.D.S.!	
"	29.1.19		Routine	
"	30.1.19		Visited A.D.S. 17 Corps. A.D.M.S. 'Q' 20 Div & 60 Bde.	
"	31.1.19		59th Inf Bde, 2nd Scot Rifles & 11th R.B.	
"	1.2			

Nelson Ward S.
D.A.D.Q. 20 Div
31.1.19

Army Form C. 2118.

WAR DIARY
or
INTELLIGENCE SUMMARY.
(Erase heading not required.)

DADOS 202

Instructions regarding War Diaries and Intelligence Summaries are contained in F. S. Regs., Part II. and the Staff Manual respectively. Title pages will be prepared in manuscript.

Place	Date	Hour	Summary of Events and Information	Remarks and references to Appendices
ACHEUX	1.2.19		Visited 20th B.M.G.C & 61st Bde H.Q.	
"	2.2.19		Routine	
"	3.2.19		Went with C.R.E. DADAG in search of site for new dump. Pending change of railhead to Doullens.	
"	4.2.19		Went to site selected with ADOS 17th Corps - Site not approved owing to insufficient space for store tents. Went all round Doullens to find accommodation, but everywhere of any size already occupied.	
"	5.2.19		Routine	
"	6.2.19		"	
"	7.2.19		Visited 61st Bde & went to Doullens re change of dump.	
"	8.2.19		92nd Bde R.F.A, Div H.Q, 6th K.S.L.I	
"	9.2.19		92nd Bde R.F.A.	
"	10.2.19		Remained at ADOS 17th Corps visited dump.	
"	11.2.19		Went to Amplier to see camps occupied by 224 & 274 BG R.G.A. with a view to taking one over. Went to Div H.Q.	
"	12.2.19		Went to Div H.Q. & A.D.O.S. 17th Corps.	
"	13.2.19		Got visits Amplier dump. 92nd Bde R.F.A.	
"	14.2.19		Visited 62nd Bde R.G.A & went to 3rd Army.	
"	15.2.19			

Army Form C. 2118.

WAR DIARY
or
INTELLIGENCE SUMMARY.
(Erase heading not required.)

Instructions regarding War Diaries and Intelligence Summaries are contained in F.S. Regs., Part II. and the Staff Manual respectively. Title pages will be prepared in manuscript.

Place	Date	Hour	Summary of Events and Information	Remarks and references to Appendices
ACHEUX	16.2.19		Routine	Yes
"	17.2.19		Went to Div HQ	Yes
"	18.2.19		Visited DDOS 3rd Army	Yes
"	19.2.19		Moved Stores to Amplier + took on Camp of 274 By R.G.A. Went to Doullens railhead	Yes
AMPLIER	20.2.19		" reminder of Stores &c from ACHEUX, went to 62nd Bde HQ + Doullens "	Yes
"	21.2.19		Ran went to Div. HQ + 62. Inf Bde.	Yes
"	22.2.19		Routine	Yes
"	23.2.19		Went to Doullens railhead + O.O. 17 C.T with A.D.O.S	Yes
"	24.2.19		" Div HQ + M.G.Bn. GOC + G.S.O.1 visited Camp	Yes
"	25.2.19		" B/91 R.F.A. O.O 17 C.Tps Div HQ.	Yes
"	26.2.19		Went to 59 Bde + O.O. 17 C.T.	Yes
"	27.2.19		Went to 11" R.B. A.D.O.S 17 Corps. O.O. 17 C.Tr. Visited DDOS 3rd Army	Yes
DOULLENS	28.2.19		Moved to Doullens + Camp of O.O. 17 C.T. Took over all XVII C.T units	Yes

Major hsp + Div
D.A.D.O.S 20. Div.

Army Form C. 2118.

WAR DIARY
or
INTELLIGENCE SUMMARY.
(Erase heading not required.)

Instructions regarding War Diaries and Intelligence Summaries are contained in F. S. Regs., Part II. and the Staff Manual respectively. Title pages will be prepared in manuscript.

Place	Date	Hour	Summary of Events and Information	Remarks and references to Appendices
DOULLENS	1-3-19		Cleared stores in Doullens, previously filled with returns.	
"	2-3-19		"	
"	3-3-19		"	
"	4-3-19		Visited Div. & Arty. HQrs.	
"	5-3-19		Went to Amiens on L.P.	
"	6-3-19		Cleared store in Doullens.	
"	7-3-19		Salved service dress (one separator in area) which I found in dump, having been	
"	8-3-19		Dumps long considerable time. Had certain of these tidied up & sent serviceable	
"	9-3-19		to base. It is suggested that Townmajors & Area Commdrs. report when such	
"	10-3-19		dumps exist so that the serviceable stores may be saved.	
"	10-3-19		D.A.D.O.S. 3rd Army visited dump.	
"	11-3-19		Visited 11th R.B.	
"	12-3-19		Went to Div. HQ	
"	13-3-19		Visited 59th Bde, 11th R.B. 20th R.W.F.C.	
"	14-3-19		61st Bde	
"	16-3-19		Inspected 2nd Leic. Rif.	
"	15-3-19		Routine.	
"	17-3-19		Went to Div. HQ	

Army Form C. 2118.

WAR DIARY
or
INTELLIGENCE SUMMARY.
(Erase heading not required.)

Instructions regarding War Diaries and Intelligence Summaries are contained in F. S. Regs., Part II. and the Staff Manual respectively. Title pages will be prepared in manuscript.

Place	Date	Hour	Summary of Events and Information	Remarks and references to Appendices
DOULLENS	18.3.19		Visited 26th M.G.C.	
"	19.3.19		Routine	
"	20.3.19		Visited 59th Bde.	
"	21.3.19		Went to Div HQ r ACHEUX re claims	
"	22.3.19		Calibration Range Frohen-le-Grand, to arrange about stores.	
"	23.3.19		Visited 25 Hy Baty 11th R.B. XVII Corps M.G.C.	
"	24		D.A.D.O.S.	
"	25		M.G.C. Calibration Range Frohen le Grand. Jewellers Ammunition Depot	
"	26		59th Bde. Issued 640 rds of top shells cartridge, 5740 rds of 18 pr from Frohen le Grand Calibration range.	
"	27		Issued 600 rounds of 4.5 shells as above. Issued different stores from dump	
"	28		Issued 342 rounds of 4.5 shells as above. Visited 11th R.B. HQs	
"	29		Visited 11th R.B. + Div D.O.	
"	30		D.D.O.S. 2nd Scottish Rifles.	
"	31		Handed over command to D.A.D.O.S. Canvas T.C.S. HQs	31.3.19

www.ingramcontent.com/pod-product-compliance
Lightning Source LLC
Chambersburg PA
CBHW081422160426
43193CB00013B/2174